Foundations of Cisco Technology 3.0
Table of Contents
Page I of VII

W9-CCJ-045

Foundations of Cisco Technology 3.0
Table of Contents
Page IV of VII

Chapter 1
Introduction to the Book

Introduction to the Book:

There are a number of concepts in the field of network technology. In most developed countries, network technology exists in almost every part of our existence. Our cars have systems which interact with cell towers. Our homes have cameras which can be activated by smart phones. We order tickets for events via a website and doctors participate in group surgery between countries via streaming video. Our civilization has truly progressed to a technology-driven society. Due to the 1960's premonitions of what the future would include, I often hear people say, "Where is my flying car?!" When I hear that sentence, I smile to myself for I know the answer to that question. It is not that the flying car has not been created, most people simply can't afford one so companies don't mass produce it.

The People Who need this book:

This book is structured in a format to allow motivated individuals to perform a number of high-order network technology tasks. Everyone whom purchases this book may not be interested in certification but simply desire to increase their knowledge in network technology. The subjects covered in this text are related to installation and maintenance of specific network technology such as Routers, Switches and Remote Access methods. The topics listed in this book are the foundation of every large network. Through the use of practical (Or what is referred to as "Hands-On") activities, the readers of this book will master the foundations of network technology and be able to perform all required tasks to implement the technology relying only on their accumulated knowledge developed through study, repetition and successful practice. The last chapter of this text entitled "Example Labs and Activities" includes many practice exercises. **The Full Videos can be found on the YouTube Channel "Foundations of Computer and Network Technologies".**

Introduction to the Field of Network Technology:

For those whom purchased this book to increase their knowledge in order to attain a certification in network technology, congratulations! You have the correct book in hand! The tasks which are displayed in the text are directly related to a number of certifications offered by Cisco and Comptia. One of the excellent aspects of understanding one vendor of network technology is the ability to "Cross-Learn" other vendor technologies. The term "IP address" is used for servers, routers, printers and cell phones. These "network device" identities are used on all of the technologies mentioned above. The only difference is "where" you would insert the settings on each platform. This book is created in a "survey-course" fashion and was developed to give the reader the ability to firmly understand network technologies and to implement them in a production environment ("Real World"). The implementation is based upon "foundation understanding" and utilization of actual technology. Persons presently working full-time in the network technology field will benefit from the tasks in this text to learn the technology in order to enhance their organization's ability and functions. Persons who desire to enter the field of network technology will benefit from developing a practical understanding of what is required for network devices to communicate and offer support services on a network or the internet.

Importance of Possessing Network Certifications:

There are a number of certifications available in the field of network technology. It is important that persons interested in the field understand the foundation of what each certification indicates in order to better position themselves in the job market. Many persons outside of the field have heard of different certifications. Certifications themselves do not make a person better at completing job tasks then someone who has no certifications. Certifications do have some essential truths to them which make their attainment highly desirable. It is regarded as true that a person who has certifications will possess the following qualities:

- **Greater knowledge of a specific technology than those without the Certification.**
    1. Persons working in the field for many years primarily know tasks and technologies which they have been exposed to via job assignment or troubleshooting situations. The unfortunate association with the learning process is that the person has not been exposed to all of the primary features of a technology. Many features can save an organization money as opposed to purchasing many other devices which provide a function that the "on-site" technology already has built into it.

- **Display of letters for hiring entity (i.e., Human Resources, Selection Committee, etc.).**
    1. Often times, the group responsible for the hiring process will not understand all the particulars surrounding the qualifications necessary to fill a technology position. In addition, after learning of all the requirements, it often becomes expensive to advertise all the desired

criteria for an application to be successful in interview selection (Often times, job advertising companies charge the company looking for applicants based upon how many words are in the advertisement (Often $1 per word, charged every week the advertisement is available in newspaper or internet format). To compensate for the "word length" of the job advertisement and the review of applications eligible for interview, hiring entities often ask their associates for a better way of advertising a position with the least amount of "words" as possible. This normally results in the hiring entity being told some technology "abbreviations" to use instead of descriptive paragraphs. Take the following scenario for example if the job announcement would cost $1 per month per word:

- **Option A:** Human Resources person creates job announcement (Total cost about $51 dollars per month):
  - ❖ The technology department needs a person who can perform the following:
    1. Install Network Operating Systems.
    2. Install, configure and troubleshoot Hubs.
    3. Install, configure and troubleshoot Switches
    4. Troubleshoot network connections on computers.
    5. Address printer problems.
    6. Answer phones on the Help Desk.
    7. Connect and install Category 5 cable in building.
    8. Connect network devices on LAN.

- **Option B:** Human Resources person creates job announcement (Total cost about $8 dollars per month):
  - ❖ The technology department needs an Net+ Certified technician.

2. Human Resources will now look for applications with the appropriate letters. Other applicants might have years of experience working on network devices. Their resumes might also list every item on the job announcement. Human Resources often look at hundreds of resumes per day, however. In fact, some companies have "Optical Character Recognition" (Often called "OCR" software which reads over all the resumes as they arrive via e-mail or posted to a job website. Human Resources attempts to be as efficient as possible, so they will only respond to those resumes which have the "Certification Letters" they were anticipating.

Examples of International Network Technology Certifications:

There are a number of certifications which are international (Valid all over the world). The certifications of these types were created by large organizations and professionals in the field of network technology. Information combined from full-time professionals, educators, and technicians was combined to create the "The Handbook of Occupational Job Titles". This document is used to identify definite and specific tasks a "Network Technology" specialist would have to perform and have knowledge. Some certifications are "vendor neutral" (Used for multiple companies and technologies) while others are "proprietary" (Offered exclusively by a specific company or organization). In order to gain industry certification, it is often required that a person pass some number of examinations or assessments hosted by the organization which sponsors the specific certification. Your desired area specialty in network technology will define which certification might be the most advantageous for you to attain. Some certifications which were active at the time of writing this book are as follows:

- **NET+ (Network+)** = Offered by a worldwide organization known as "CompTIA (Computer Technicians International Association). The Net+ often viewed as a "survey" certification. The primary focus of the certification is "Concepts and Knowledge". The certification examination assesses multiple terms existing in network technology from the perspective of many different devices from multiple companies. The examination does not focus on any single technology or process from start to finish. This is often viewed as the "Entry Level" network technology certification.
- **CCT (Cisco Certified Technician)** = Introduction Certification highlighting support and maintenance of routers and switches. Persons with this certification can use the Cisco Internetwork Operating System and the Cisco Command Line Interface (CLI). Classification of IP Addressing, subnetting and security are also aspects of this certification.
- **CCENT (Cisco Certified Entry-Level Networking Technician)** = These professionals have the ability to service and maintain small enterprise networks and have a familiarity with basic network security. Objectives for this certification include network technology fundamentals, security and wireless concepts, routing and switching. The exam for the CCENT is also 50% of the exams required for the CCNA certification (This exam scheduled for discontinuation in 2020).

- **CCNA (Cisco Certified Network Associate)** = This certification is designed to assess the skills of Network Administrator and Engineers with 1-3 years of experience. The objectives of the exam(s) include the ability to configure, operate and troubleshoot various network technologies in a medium to large sized network environments. To gain this certification, it is possible to take either one exam or a two-part exam (Passing the first exam renders a person a CCENT, passing the 2nd exam will render a person also a CCNA.

How to Earn a Network Technology Certification:

There are many certifications which indicate various levels of knowledge in Network Technology. This text seeks to offer the foundation knowledge which would supplement a program of study for those desiring to achieve some of those network technology certifications. At the time of the writing of this book, the following are some of the certifications available in the field of network technology:

- **Self-Study and Simulators:**
    1. In order to get certified, there are no mandated courses, colleges or training programs. In fact, many certified people have never taken a computer class. Essentially, they were "Self-Taught" after locating resources which would allow them to accumulate the knowledge to pass specific certification examinations. Suggested resources would be the following:
        - **Simulators** = These are a practical tool which allow practicing many high-order tasks required on network technology. There is no "best" software for each has features which might be advantages for some certifications while not necessary for others. Some simulation software titles would include the following:
            - Boson NetSim (Boson.com)
            - Packet Tracer (Cisco.com)
            - GNS3 (GNS3.com)
            - CCIE Lab Builder (Cisco.com)
            - Virtual Box (Oracle.com)
        - **Certification Textbooks** = These are produced by many different publishers. The book you are presently reading is actually an example of the type used to earn certification. Due to the many authors in computer

technology, it would be difficult to say which book is the "best" but there are some methods you can use to select the books which are best for your certification endeavors. The following are a few ideas:

- Talk to technology professionals who have certifications. They can tell you which books and/or simulation software they used to pass the exams.
- As "technology training" programs which books they use. Often time you can purchase the books without taking the classes.
- Certification Organization Websites (i.e., "Comptia.com", "Microsoft.com" and "Cisco.com" often have links to books recommended for certifications. Be sure to check which numbers are associated with each exam prior to purchasing the books. Often books are sold which are associated with "old" and "Outdated" exams which are still using the same name.

- **Network Technology Training Schools:**
  1. Presently, there are many "For-Profit" institutions which have training programs and even degrees advertised as either "Network Technology Certificates" and even "Network Technology Degrees". Often times, these schools are called "Career Training Education (CTE)" institutions. These programs possess a broad variety of learning objectives and standards. When selecting a network technology program, do research on what standards they use to create the program. Questions such as the following would be beneficial when evaluating a potential program:
     - ➢ What colleges or universities will accept the classes and credits from this program?
     - ➢ What is the cost for this program compared to other schools both "For-Profit" and "Not-For-Profit"?
     - ➢ What standards were used to establish the program?
     - ➢ What organizations accredit the program?
     - ➢ Please show me your job placement statistics.

> ➢ Am I allowed to re-take classes for free after completion of the program to keep skills up to date?

- **Two and Four-Year Colleges and Universities:**
  1. Over the last 10 years, many colleges and universities have created "Network Technology" programs. The advantage to these colleges is that they also confer college degrees which would make a person more marketable in the technology field. In addition, having a degree allows a person to apply for other jobs outside of the field of network technology if they decided to change careers or needed employment until that perfect "Technology" job becomes available.

There are many institutions available which offer outstanding training experiences. Their costs range from free to extremely expensive, however. Do your research and balance out elements such as your available time and finances. Often times, certificate programs are a good place for basic understanding with the expectation that industry wide certification may follow in the future.

Recommendation on Correct Order to Take Certification Examinations:

Although it is not a requirement, having more than one certification is highly advantageous to a network professional. Multiple certifications will show perspective employers that a technician is an expert in many areas. If a technician had both a MCP and a CCENT, they know this person can both create a network and repair all the computers which are attached to the network. Many persons in the network technology field have a perspective on which examinations should be taken first and the particular order in which they should be attempted. There is no concrete document for most certifications attempts but there are some practical theories on the process. When planning on which certification(s) to take and their correct order, give thought the following:

- **What jobs do you have interest?** = If a person wants to work on networks and has no desire to repair computers, there is no need to take the A+. Simply stick with examinations such as "Net+", "CCENT", etc.
- **Which certification will make later certifications easier to achieve?** = Many certifications have similar objectives. Examples of similar test objectives would be such as the following certifications which all have similar questions:

- Net+
- CCT
- CCENT.

Taking the examinations which have similar subject matter will make future examinations easier. It is like studying once to pass three different tests. There is no definite order of examinations at the lower levels of certification. Simply select the exams that will benefit you the greatest in the smallest amount of time.

Chapter 2
Network Technology Groups and Organizations

Network Technology Groups and Organizations:

In addition to the specifics and details of connecting network devices, there are a number of "theories" and "Concepts" which are not "hands-on" elements. Prior to many of the technologies used in network design, there were many groups and organizations which discussed methods of communication, terms and standards. Many of these organizations are the primary contact point for network technologies and many of their discussions have become the standards used worldwide. The following terms reflect some of the groups and theories which are highly utilized and well known in the field of network technology:

- **RFC** = (Request for Comments) is the general name for a document which is disseminated and discussed by multiple groups and organizations. These organizations are normally international and reflect primary groups of representatives in various areas of technology. Examples would be the Institute of Electrical and Electronics Engineer (IEEE) and the International Organization for Standardization (ISO). Each organization modifies the document, adding and subtracting statements, descriptions and categories. After an agreed amount of time, the organizations vote on the RFC and it is adopted as a "Standard". A "Standard" is a recommendation on how a product, function or activity should occur. It is not a legal rule, simply a guideline implemented to increase clarity and to reduce the amount of documentation which would have to accompany a product. The guidelines are then published by groups such as the Internet Engineering Task Force (IETF) and the Internet Society (ISOC), two of the primary organizations which establish standards for internet and computer technology communications. Some examples of RFC's include the following:

Request for Comment Examples	
RFC 20	ASCII format for network interchange
RFC 1518	Address allocation with CIDR
RFC 1542	DHCP/BOOTP complient routers
RFC 792	Internet control message protocol
RFC 1034	Domain names - concepts and facilities
RFC 1058	Routing information protocol
RFC 1459	Internet relay chat protocol

- **ISO** = (International Organization for Standardization) is an independent, non-governmental international organization based in Geneva, Switzerland. The participants of the ISO are considered to be experts who share knowledge and develop voluntary international standards to support innovation, consistency and global solutions to various worldwide situations. The members include over 161 national groups who all discuss, devise and develop standards for products, services and systems concerning quality and safety. There are over 21,000 International Standards and related ISO documents ranging from technology, food, energy, waste and many other areas. There are two primary models of communications in networking which are advocated by the ISO:

  1. **OSI Model (Open Systems Interconnect)** = A conceptual description listing the elements of network devices and how they communicate. This model separates network communication, software and devices into 7 distinct layers. Each layer supports specific functions which in turn allow transition into layers either above or below it. Without going into detail, the following the seven layers of the OSI model and some of the related features within the layer:

OPEN SOURCE INTERCONNECT (OSI-MODEL)				
LAYER#	NAME	FUNCTION	ASSOCIATION	PDU TYPE
7	APPLICATION	File transfer, e-mail	Browsers ms-outlook	DATA
6	PRESENTATION	Formats data for transfer	Ansi, oem, etc.	DATA
5	SESSION	Creates and coordinates connections between applications		DATA
4	TRANSPORT	Data flow and error correction	Tcp, udp	SEGMENT
3	NETWORK	Establishes communication path between nodes	Routers	PACKET
2	DATA	Conversion to bits	Switches	FRAME
1	PHYSICAL	Carries the bits	Hubs, nic's, cables	BIT
WAYS TO REMEMBER LAYERS ORDER (First letter of each word represents layer:				
ALL PIMPS SELECT THE NICE DIAMOND PIECES				
ALL PEOPLE SEEM TO NEED DATA PROCESSING				
PLEASE DO NOT THROW SAUSAGE PIZZA AWAY				

  2. **TCP/IP Model (Originally called the "DOD Model")** = This communication model separates network communications into 4

layers. Essentially, this model predates the OSI model and did not originally include much "software" related specifications (In the 60's, there were no applications such as "Firefox" and "Microsoft Word" so most communication technology was related to hardware). As time progressed, layers representing software were encompassed in the higher levels of the TCP/IP model. Below is a representation of the TCP/IP model as related to the OSI model:

TCP/IP MODEL		
LAYER#	NAME	FUNCTION
4	APPLICATION	FTP, Telnet, e-mail, DNS
3	TRANSPORT (HOST-TO-HOST)	Formats data for transfer
2	INTERNET	Creates and coordinates connections between applications
1	NETWORK	Data flow and error correction

- **IEEE (Institute of Electrical and Electronics Engineer)** = Members include thousands of professionals working in the field of electronics, networking, computers and overall science technology. With its beginning in about 1844, IEEE is often considered to be the world's largest technical "Think Tank". Some of the standards implemented by IEEE include the following:

IEEE Standards	
Section Name	**Brief Reference Description**
IEEE 802.1	**Higher Layer LAN Protocols**
IEEE 802.2	**LLC**

IEEE 802.3	Ethernet
IEEE 802.4	Token bus
IEEE 802.5	Token ring MAC layer
IEEE 802.6	MAN's
IEEE 802.7	Broadband LAN using Coaxial Cable
IEEE 802.8	Fiber Optic TAG
IEEE 802.9	Integrated Services LAN
IEEE 802.10	Interoperable LAN Security
IEEE 802.11	Wireless LAN (WLAN) & Mesh (Wi-Fi Certification)
IEEE 802.12	100BaseVG
IEEE 802.13	None according to records
IEEE 802.14	Cable modems
IEEE 802.15	Wireless PAN
IEEE 802.15.1	Bluetooth certification

Chapter 3
Concepts, Devices and Signals
in Network Technology

Selected Concepts, Devices and Signals in Network Technology:

In the field of network technology, there are a number of terms utilized for descriptions, settings and configuration. Prior to the exploration of the different technologies, it will be helpful to give a brief overview of a few of the concepts a person will encounter and have to manipulate. The following are a few of the terms and explanations which will be discussed in this text:

- **Bandwidth** = This term describes the maximum amount of data which can exist on a connection at the same time. Contemporary network devices operate at one of four speeds: 10, 100, 1000 or 10,000 Mbps. If devices of different speeds are directly connected the "faster" port will reduce its speed to match the speed of the "slower" port. Please note, although the speeds are very distinct, an active connection only uses a portion of the available port speed. Think of it as a garden hose which has a "trickle" of water passing thru it at one time while other times the faucet is fully turned on and the entire inside of the hose is filled with water traveling towards the spout.

- **Protocol Data Units** = Depending on the type of network and software in use, technicians will describe the "message pieces" differently. Networks have equipment which requires the messages to be formatted in many different ways to be compatible with other network devices. Below are some of the more widely used terms to describing network technology messages along with generic descriptions to be expanded upon later:
  - ➤ **Packets** = Small information units. Very fast and compatible with multiple types of networks.
  - ➤ **Frames** = Think of a frame as a collection of "packets" in a container. The container allows groups of packets to have rules of travel and elements of security to protect the data.
  - ➤ **Cells** = Imagine this as a bubble or circle which carries large amounts of data. Cells were used on older networks and recent Video-Related networks because the data was more reliable concerning arriving at destinations.
  - ➤ **Tokens** = This would be regarded as a "Cell" with rules. A Token is configured to travel in a specific direction between intermediate destinations arranged on a network. The token always uses the same path and often has path-redundancy in case the primary route is cut or damaged.

- **"Amount", "Units" and "Speeds" in networks** = There are many descriptions which attempts to define maximum amount of data with the longest time it takes for a message unit to travel from a source to a destination. This is specified by the type of technology the message is using to travel. There are various types of networks technology, each with specific distance advantages and limitations. In this book, we include discussions which reflect the following speed format:
  - **bps** = Bits per second.
  - **Kbps** = Kilobits per second (Equal to 1000bps).
  - **Mbps** = Megabits per second (Equal to 1000kbps).
  - **Gbps** = Gigabits per second (Equal to 1000Mbps).
- **Transmission Types** = Essentially, there are two general signal forms which are illustrated and measured differently:
  - **Broadband** = The measure of this form normally is illustrated with a smooth curving line which rises and falls like a "camel's back". This is measured using a concept called "Frequency". Frequency is the time that passes before an event occurs as well as the position of the line between the occurrences. The carrier for broadband is normally light waves or sound waves.
  - **Baseband** = The measure of this form is illustrated by using sharp, straight lines which travel up or down with pauses traveling from left to right. Think of this as something which looks like a "Picket Fence" or the top of the chess game piece called a "Rook". The carrier for this type of signal is often electrical "pops" that register as either "on" or "off".
  - **Wireless** = Wireless networks exist between nodes which use the "air" as a medium. Clients transmit and receive either "light/sound/or radio" waves for communication. Some popular wireless technologies are the following:
    - ❖ **Bluetooth** = Very popular connection technologies used in cars, cell phones, entertainment systems, etc. Bluetooth requires very little equipment and operates on very low power. The range for Bluetooth networks vary from 33 feet to 10 meters depending on the class device in use.
    - ❖ **NFC (Near Field Communication)** = NFC allows devices such as a smartphones, printers and computers to communicate. The primary limitation of NFC is the range. Basic NFC requires the devices to be within about 2 inches of each other for communication. This type of

technology is often used to allow two cell phones to transmit data between them if they are held close together.

❖ **802.11 Standards** = These are documents which discuss and illustrate recommended methods of wireless communications which were created by the Institute of Electrical and Electronics Engineers (IEEE) LAN/MAN Standards Committee (Also called "IEEE 802"). There are a number of versions of the "802.11" many of which began in the mid-1990's. Some of the more better-known standards include the following:

Standard	Frequency	Maximum Throughput	Distance (Radius)
802.11a	5 GHz	54 Mbit/s	115 feet (Obstruction limited)
802.11b	2.4 GHz	11 Mbit/s	115 feet
802.11g	2.4 GHz	54 Mbit/s	125 feet
802.11n	5GHz and/or 2.4GHz	300 Mbit/s	230 feet (Obstruction limited)

- **VoIP Phones** = Instead of using a system called "POTS (Plain old Telephone System)" which requires the installation of telephone lines, there are technologies which allow telephones to be connected to traditional computer networks. These phones use the same software which allows computers to interact with networks. The networks which accept these types of phones are often referred to as "Voice over Internet Protocol" networks. Many telecommunication companies include VoIP as services they offer such as Vonage, Comcast, Cisco and others.
- **Network-Based computers** = In order to store and retrieve data on the internet requires the use of computers called "Servers". These computers hold and display movies, text, photos and many other products and services used in the world. We also discuss a type of computer called a "client" or "workstation". Clients are simply computer-related devices which primarily access the data on servers. Examples of clients would be your home computer or a Smartphone.
- **Hubs** = This device is one of the oldest used in networks. This device essentially multiplies physical connections to a network. For example, if there is normally a single connection which leads to the internet in a building. The hub would allow multiple devices access

to this single connection. The devices could be computers, printers, or even video cameras. We normally classify hubs as "legacy devices". A legacy device is something that is based upon older technology but is still often used today. When selecting to use a Hub on a network, there are a few "Pros" and "Cons" which should be considered:

> **Pros:**
1. **Inexpensive** = Hubs are often sold for under $60 dollars for small home offices.
2. **Easy to use** = No configuration required. Simply plug in the ports and electricity and they operate.
3. **Widely available** = Due to the number of years they have been around, they can be found thru any network technology supplier.

> **Cons**:
1. **Divides bandwidth** = Each device you plug in will reduce the bandwidth the hub is rated to support. Take the following example:
   a. A hub which operates at 10Mbps has 10 available ports.
      i. If two devices are connected, the hub now runs at 5Mbps.
      ii. If ten devices are connected, the hub now runs at 1Mbps.
2. **Requires close physical proximity for repair** = Traditionally, there is no way to access, maintain or repair a standard, base-model hub unless you can touch it. If a person's office is on the 4th floor of a building but the connection leads to the hub in the basement, someone will have to walk to the basement to address the hubs fault.
3. **Single-port signal** = Essentially one unit of data can pass thru the hub at a given time (Please note that this is in "milliseconds"). While that single data unit passes thru a single port in the hub, no other transmissions can occur on the other ports.

- **Switches** = This device operates much like a hub except it compensates for some of the disadvantages associated with hubs. The prices for switches range from moderate to extremely expensive (Some models cost $8,000.00 or more). The following are some aspects concerning switches:

- ➤ **Multiplies network connections** = One port is normally connected to the network while dozens of others are connected to other network devices (Hubs, Switches, etc.) or computer systems (Servers, clients, printers, phones, etc.).
- ➤ **Dedicated bandwidth** = No bandwidth is divided due to connected devices. Regardless the number of physical connections, switches will maintain the bandwidth for which they are rated.
- ➤ **Multiple lines of simultaneous communications** = Switches allow multiple signals or communications to travel thru the devices at essentially the same time.
- ➤ **Remote access** = A switch can be configured to allow connections from anywhere in the world as long as it has an ip address and electricity being supplied. There are multiple methods of "remote access" utilized on switches and other network devices.
- ➤ **Network Segmentation** = Mid-range and higher switches have the ability to separate and segregate section of a network. This process is called "VLANs (Virtual Local Area Networks)". Some VLAN implementations are for the following:
  1. **Security** = Assuring specific groups of computers cannot interact with other computers (i.e., student computers versus teacher computers).
  2. **Bandwidth conservation** = A single computer uploading or downloading large files can hamper a network. If you segment the network with VLANs, only computers on that particular VLAN would be hampered. Operations on the other computers would occur because they do not know the other VLANs exist.
- • **Routers** = These network devices are the primary connection points of the internet. Essentially, each building which has an internet connection normally has all of the switches connected in series terminating into a Router. The router provides the connection to an Internet Service Provider (ISP) which is connected to the internet backbone (Really the Department of Defense for which every country you presently reside). In addition to the primary internet connection, Routers also provide the following functions:
  - ➤ **Remote Access** = A Router can be configured to allow connections from anywhere in the world as long as it has an ip address and electricity being supplied. There are multiple

methods of "remote access" utilized on routers and other network devices.

> **Filtering** = Signals on the internet constantly travel and will attempt to flow into networks for which they are not destined. Routers will block any communications which attempt to access a network in which the desired target does not exist.

> **Traffic Flow** = The internet is a large, complicated set of interconnected pathways. Routers can learn the fastest routes between sending and receiving devices. In addition, when a pathway fails, routers have the ability to negotiate with other routing devices to find other ways to destinations. Routers are often regarded as the "Traffic Cops" of the internet.

Cables and Connections:

All network devices are connected in some format. The actual connections are all over the world. Sometimes deep underground, some undersea and others going well above the earth to return to a remote destination. The various network connections use metal wires, "glass-like" fibers while others can communicate through the air without being physically connected. In conversations concerning network technology another way of saying "connection type" is "media" or "medium". Various media has different connectors, lengths, advantages and disadvantages. The following are some of the media used in various types of networks.

- **Network Interface Card (NIC)** = This term often describes the internal portion on a computer which controls connections to a network through the use of some type of connection media which could be metal, fiber or wireless.
- **Port** = This term describes the connection point into a NIC or interface on switch or router.
- **Coax** = (Short for "Coaxial Cable") is one of the oldest network technology media. This cable has been used since the late 60's. More recently Coax is used primarily in visual implementations such as CCTV (Closed Circuit Television). A version of it is also used by some cable television carriers to connect a home modem or "Home Router" to the demarc in the house (The hole in the wall which connects to your ISP (Internet Service Provider). Coax comes in the two following versions:
  > **ThickNet** = Cabling of this type is older and not used frequently. It can be found connecting older buildings within

corporate complexes, libraries or universities. ThickNet is about 1/2 inch in diameter and one of its major disadvantages was that it was not very flexible. The primary transmission speed most ThickNet networks achieved was up to 10 Mbps with a maximum single length of no more than 500 meters (Approximately 1,640 feet). ThickNet is often referred to as 10Base5 (The maximum distance of a segment equals 500 meters so it was agreed upon to drop the last two zeros).

> **ThinNet** = ThinNet resembles the type of wire which is often used to connect home subscriber's television to cable boxes TV. ThinNet coax is about 1/4 inch in diameter and is more flexible then ThickNet. The longest span of a ThinNet cable is 185 meters (607ft). When describing this cable, it is often referred to as 10Base2 (Persons in the field desired to "abbreviate" the name for the technology. Since the maximum distance is 185 meters, it was agreed upon to "round the 185 up" to "200" and then drop the two zeros). This type of network media uses a connector called a "BNC (Bayonet Neill Concelman)".

• **Category Cable (Also called Twisted Pair or "Cat")** = Cable of this type is what we often see connected to telephones or basic network devices. The normal distance limitation of category cable is about 100 meters (Approximately 328 feet). The other name "twisted-pair" originates from the construction of the cable. Within the cable, there are multiple-pairs of wires which are twisted in parallel (Side-by-side).

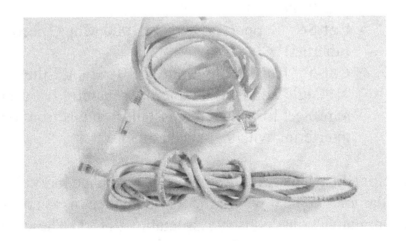

- There are many definitions concerning twisted pair cabling. One definition is based on the material used in the cable creation. Below appear the three primary material types:
  - **Shielded Twisted Pair (STP)** = Metallic foil surrounds the twisted wire pairs within the cable. The foil increases protection against electromagnetic interference which allows for faster data transmissions. STP is sometimes more expensive due to its composition and devices which might be required to provide better protection against EMI such as termination and grounding.
  - **Unshielded Twisted (UTP)** = Cable of this type has no layer of material specifically provided for protection. It is often the type of cable viewed directly connected to computers from a hub or a switch.
  - **Plenum-Rated** = This type of cable incorporates special materials in the cable covering. The makeup of the cable includes flame-retardant synthetics and low smoke materials to provide increased resistance against fire or the emission of toxic gasses.
- **Category Cable Specifications** = Different versions of category cable have numbers which indicate their use. Below are some of the category types:
  - **Cat-1 thru 3** = Primarily telephones and older basic network technology.
  - **Cat-4** = Supported speeds of 16 Mbps
  - **Cat-5** = Supports speeds of between 10/100 Mbps (Called "FastEthernet).
  - **Cat-5e** = Supports speeds of 1000 Mbps speeds (Called Gigabit Ethernet)
  - **Cat-6** = It's suitable for up to 10 gigabit Ethernet (Called "10GigE") and has an internal separator between pairs of wires to protect from signal crosstalk (Signals from one set of wires interfering with signals on other wires).

- **Wire Specifications for Category** = Cables have individual wires in a particular arrangement within the RJ-45 connector as specified by Telecommunications Industry Association (TIA). These arrangements of wires allow specific communications between network devices and have particular names such as 568A and 568B as illustrated below:

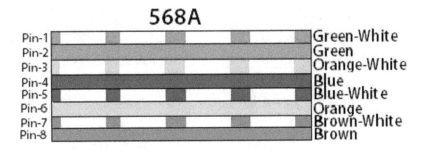

568A

Pin-1	Green-White
Pin-2	Green
Pin-3	Orange-White
Pin-4	Blue
Pin-5	Blue-White
Pin-6	Orange
Pin-7	Brown-White
Pin-8	Brown

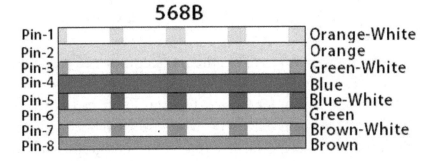

568B

Pin-1	Orange-White
Pin-2	Orange
Pin-3	Green-White
Pin-4	Blue
Pin-5	Blue-White
Pin-6	Green
Pin-7	Brown-White
Pin-8	Brown

Notice that the primary difference from 568A is the wires placed in Pins 1, 2 and 6.

- **Terms for Cables with Specific Wiring Arrangements** = Depending on what the cable is connecting will dictate the wiring arrangement which also has a term to describe the cable. The following are often used cables in network technology:
  - ➢ **Straight-Cable** = This cable has both ends configured with one wiring scheme (Either 568A or 568B). This is a type of category cable which is used to connect dissimilar devices in the following manner.
    1. Computer to Hub or Switch
    2. Switch to Router
  - ➢ **Crossover Cable** = This cable has each end configured with one a different wiring scheme (568A on one end and 568B on the other). This cable is used to connect similar devices such as in the following:
    1. Switch to Switch
    2. Router to Router
    3. Computer to Router (Not very frequently but can be done)
  - ➢ **Rolled Cable** = This cable traditionally has a 568A standard but it is reversed on one end of the cable (Exact opposite on

both ends). Also, this cable is normally "flat" and might be "light-blue" or "black" in color. Rolled cables are used for "Configuration" of devices and not network "Communications". Also, this cable normally has an "adaptor" on it so it **can be connected to a "serial" interface on a computer.**

➢ **Console Cable** = This a enhanced rolled cable but one end has the adaptor hard wired (Connected) to it. Traditionally, this cable is "flat" and "light-blue" in color.

- **Fiber-Optic Cable** = This media is comprised of an almost hair thin material referred to as "Glass" which is encased in mirrored cladding and a protective outer sleeve. Optical Fiber has become a highly preferred media in use on networks regardless of if there in a single building or covering large expanses of geographic territory. There are a number of advantages in the use of fiber optic media such as the following:

  1. Carry signals further than copper media.
  2. Not susceptible to electromagnetic or radio interference.
  3. Faster transmission speeds than copper media.
  4. Higher bandwidth availability than other media types.
  5. Physical weight of media.

Essentially, signals of light travel thru fiber allowing incredibly fast speeds (Upwards of 10,000 Mbps). It also allows communications over long distances (2 kilometers and greater). Fiber media comes in a multitude of specifications which support different technologies. In addition, fiber cables also have various terminators allowing their connections to various network appliances. Due to its construction fiber-optic cable is very expensive. A full discussion of fiber optic technologies exceed the requirements of this publication but there are some aspects which may prove beneficial to a network professional. One of the aspects is the conversation of "single-mode" versus "multimode". Although there are many type of fiber-optic cable, two will receive attention in this text:

➢ **Multi-mode** = 550 meters
➢ **Single-Mode** = support runs between 2 meters and 10,000 meters

To develop an understanding of the characteristics of fiber, we can use a number of analogies. To give an example of the different technologies simply imagine a street in any city. Some roads allow a single vehicle to travel in one direction or the other. Since there is only one primary line of travel there is the potential of traffic jams at specific intersections. In this scenario, there is only one path of travel that can be used at a given time. This would be an example of "single-mode". Taking the example onto its next progression, many cities have major streets and highways which not only allow vehicles to travel in two directions at the same time but there are also multiple lanes on the highway. The multiple lanes allow many vehicles to travel in both directions thereby reducing the likelihood of traffic jams. Due to the increased number of lanes and the reduction of traffic jams there more vehicles which can transport persons and products simultaneously between multiple sources and destinations. This would be an example of "multimode". Fiber cable terminal ends vary in construction. Regardless of being single-mode or multimode there are several specifications of fiber as well as terminators associated with them. Some of the more well-known are cable types and terminators such as "SFP" and "1000BASE-X". "Small Form-factor Pluggable (SFP)" is a category of fiber terminator which support various types of connections to network devices. 1000BASE-X is a category of connection associated with either fiber optic or copper media which supports connection speeds of 1000 megabits per second (Also called Gigabit). Depending on both the transceiver (Terminator) and the cable used provides different distances and capabilities as in the following examples:

> **1000BASE-SX** = Supports expanses up to 550 meters traditionally utilized on multimode. This type of cable is often used in vertical runs ("Between floors") in large multi-floor buildings.

> **1000BASE-LX** = Traditionally used for moderate geographic WAN distances between buildings with ranges up to 10 kilometers (A little over 6 miles) over single-mode fiber. When an "SX" type of terminator is used on multimode the distance reduces to a usual limitation of about 550 meters (About 1800 feet).

> **1000BASE-LH** = Traditionally used for a long geographic WAN distances between buildings with ranges up to 70 kilometers (A little over 43½ miles) over single-mode fiber.

Some types which might be found on a fiber-based network include the following:

> **Straight Tip Connector (ST)**

> **Standard Connector (SC)**

> **Lucent Connector (LC)**

> **Small Form Factor Pluggable (SFP)**

Combining Cable and Speed Technologies as Descriptions:

Multiple types of technologies are combined for the functioning of most networks. Although people often use the term "Ethernet" cable, understand that this is a technology "norm" and not a thoroughly complete descriptor. There are however, other terms used in technology which combines many aspects of how a network functions. These terms are actually technology field standards. The following is a brief description of some technologies prevalent in network technology:

- **10Base5** = Network which used RG-8 cable media about .50 inches in diameter with baseband transmissions of up to 10 megabits per second (Mbps). The primary connectors were called "AUI (Attachment User Interface)". The maximum distance between nodes is 500 meters (About 1,640 feet). Another name which was used for this type of network was "ThickNet". This is an older technology which is not used very often due to the materials being very expensive but can still be found as the "Backbone" cable on networks due to its durability and distance capacity.
- **10Base2** = Networks of this type use .25 thick RG-58A/U coaxial cable terminated with BNC connectors. The maximum speed is up to 10Mbps using baseband transmissions for a range of 185 meters (About 607 feet) per segment. A name used for this type of network was also "ThinNet". The "2" is intended to reflect the number "185" rounded up to "200" and dropping the last two zeros in order to make the description easier to pronounce.
- **10BaseT** = Using "Category" cable, these networks support 10 Mbps over two pairs of copper wires within a cable which can house multiple pairs of wires. The maximum segment is 100 meters (About 328 feet). This network type utilizes RJ-45 connectors. In this description the letter "T" represents that idea that the cable type uses very small wires "twisted" in pairs.
- **1000Base-T** = Using "Category" cable, these networks support either 10, 100, or 1000 Mbps over four pairs of highly twisted cable utilizing better copper and often times transistors in NIC's. The maximum segment is 100 meters (About 328 feet). This network type utilizes RJ-45 connectors. In this description the letter "T" represents that idea that the cable type uses very small wires "twisted" in pairs.
- **Hop (Or "Hop Count")** = Network term which describes the number of devices a PDU must travel through in order to arrive at its destination. Any device which makes a decision about which path messages take is

included in a "hop count". Devices which have no routing abilities (i.e., hub, server, etc.) are not included in a hop count.

Corporate and Industry Network Connection Types:

Large organizations and companies often require extremely high speeds and bandwidths to allow offices, buildings and even large corporate campuses to handle business and other various transactions over extreme distances across the earth. Over the last twenty years, the internet has revolutionized how businesses operate Internet Service Providers to modify, expand and increase their capabilities to support their customers. The following is a list of the standards often which have been used by ISP's regarding the type of connection technology as well as the bandwidth and speed each supported:

Connection Definition	Maximum Bandwidth and Speed
T1 (23+1 Channels)	1.544 Mbps
T2 (96 Channels)	6.312 Mbps
T3 (672 Channels)	44.736 Mbps
E3 (Europian)	34.368 Mbps
OC-1 (Optical Carrier)	51.84 Mbps
OC-9 (Optical Carrier)	466.56 Mbps
OC-24 (Optical Carrier)	1.244 Gbps
OC-768 (Optical Carrier)	39.813 Gbps

Protocols (Network Language for Communications):

Regardless of what type of device is on a network, there must be software to allow it to be managed and to allow it to communicate. The names of some of these software's are often used to describe what makes up the primary communication standard of a network. The following protocol types below are some highlights of the software which allows networks to communicate:

- **IPX/SPX (Internet Packet Exchange/Sequential Packet Exchange)** = This is a LAN communication protocol developed by one of the original companies for network communications known as Novell networks. This protocol uses hexadecimal identities (0-9 and A-F) for devices and cannot be routed on the internet.
- **TCP/IP (Transmission Control Protocol/Internet Protocol)** = Method for communications between computers on small and large networks. The protocol is actually a combination TCP/IP is a combination of two protocols suites verbally separated for easier explanation. Each suite is a

combination of protocols but they have the same purposes as in the following:

1. **Transmission Control Protocol (TCP)** = Attempts to assure the dependable transmission of data between networks and devices. Within this capacity, the protocol will attempt to correct for data errors and requests re-transmissions of lost data.
2. **Internet Protocol (IP)** = Attempts to define the path that data, signals, packets, pdu's, etc., will take to travel between a sending device and destination.

- **IPv4 (Internet Protocol Version 4)** = The primary protocol in data communication over different kinds of networks. This protocol identifies network devices by a 12-character decimal identity separated into 4 sections (192.168.1.1). Using this system allowed a worldwide network with over four billion IP addresses. With the increase of internet-connected devices (i.e., cell phones, car and home security, etc.) however, there is the potential of running out of IP's which can be accessed over the internet. Due to the address limitation, networks presently use other identity methods including IPv6, CIDR and VLSM (Terms will be explained and described later in this text).
- **IPv5 (Known as "Internet Streaming Protocol")** = This was primarily used for transmitting video and direct communication between routing devices for services for routing. Extremely fast and robust with multiple applications but requires high-end network devices for implementation.
- **IPv6 (Internet Protocol Version 6)** = This utilizes a combination of 32 hexadecimal characters for the identity of network devices. An example of an IPv6 identity would be "fe80::75ea:6ec0:e6f8:f037". This method allows close to 340 undecillion available IP addresses. IPv6 also understands communications from IPv4 devices. Unfortunately, IPv4 devices cannot understand communications directly from IPv6 networks unless there is a software or device between the different networks to provide data conversion.
- **DHCP (Dynamic Host Configuration Protocol)** = This protocol gives identities to network devices in the form of an IPv4 address. The protocol will also provide network settings so network devices can find networks outside of the specific LAN. DHCP also attempts to assure that duplicated IP addresses are not given out to multiple network devices which could cause an entire network to stop functioning.
- **DNS (Domain Name System (or Service or Server))** = This associates domain names into IP addresses. Whenever someone wants to go to

"Disney.com" the request goes to DNS servers around the world. Those servers have a "Shared list" which includes all known domains linked to IP addresses. Once the domain is found in the DNS server, the IP address is sent to the computer which requested the domain. The computer then uses that address to get to the desired domain.

- **Telnet** = This is a protocol which uses a "Command Line Interface" which allows connection to network devices (Routers, Switches, Computers, etc.) over vast TCP/IP distances. Options for use include browsing directors and limited "Text-based" control over devices. Although very effective, telnet is highly unsecure for PDU's are easily read with widely available software.
- **SSH (Secure Shell)** = This protocol allows authentication and hides (Also called "Encrypts") communications between two or more devices when connected over public or less-secure environments like the Internet. Many network administrators use this for remotely accessing network systems and computers in order to perform commands or transmit and receive files.
- **TFTP (Trivial File Transfer Protocol)** = This is a protocol and software suite used for moving small files between devices which do not have overhead or the need for security or authentication.

Ports of Communications:

Earlier in this book, there is the mention of "protocols" which are simply "rules of communication" between network devices. Some of the protocols listed were "DHCP", "Telnet" and "HTTP". As long as network devices are using similar protocols, they will have the ability to communicate and/or exchange data. There are other elements related to network communications, however. These other elements are classified as "Ports".

"Port" is a term used to identify a logical, software path between devices. Whatever media (Cable, wireless, etc.) software uses to travel is not a single cable in function. In actuality, there are 65,535 different paths of communications available between any devices communicating on a network. The following diagram is an example using "DHCP", "HTTP" and "Telnet":

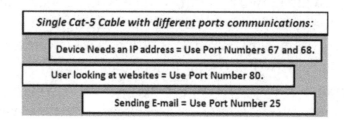

Single Cat-5 Cable with different ports communications:

Device Needs an IP address = Use Port Numbers 67 and 68.

User looking at websites = Use Port Number 80.

Sending E-mail = Use Port Number 25

Any or all of these ports can be used at any given time. Different types of software are configured to communicate on different ports. The picture below displays different communications occurring on a computer which is presently viewing "Disney.com". The command used in the command line interface (CLI) after visiting the website is "netstat –a". There are a number of ports which display "Disney.com" related entries. Each of the entries which reflect "website" communications will display as an IP address with a "colon (:)" followed with "HTTP" and "HTTPS":

```
TCP    192.168.1.118:63508    server-54-192-36-235:http   LAST_ACK
TCP    192.168.1.118:63510    ec2-54-243-80-169:http      LAST_ACK
TCP    192.168.1.118:63511    server-54-192-36-125:http   LAST_ACK
TCP    192.168.1.118:63512    server-54-192-36-125:http   LAST_ACK
TCP    192.168.1.118:63513    server-54-192-36-125:http   LAST_ACK
TCP    192.168.1.118:63521    server-54-192-36-125:http   LAST_ACK
TCP    192.168.1.118:63527    server-54-192-36-235:http   LAST_ACK
TCP    192.168.1.118:63537    133:http                    LAST_ACK
TCP    192.168.1.118:63539    192.229.210.12:http         LAST_ACK
TCP    192.168.1.118:63540    ec2-52-27-8-169:http        TIME_WAIT
TCP    192.168.1.118:63541    ec2-184-73-198-200:http     TIME_WAIT
TCP    192.168.1.118:63545    ec2-52-205-153-11:http      TIME_WAIT
TCP    192.168.1.118:63546    ec2-54-88-194-5:https       ESTABLISHED
TCP    192.168.1.118:63547    192.229.210.12:http         LAST_ACK
TCP    192.168.1.118:63548    192.229.210.12:http         LAST_ACK
TCP    192.168.1.118:63550    ec2-54-88-194-5:http        TIME_WAIT
TCP    192.168.1.118:63552    a184-26-44-105:http         LAST_ACK
TCP    192.168.1.118:63552
```

The Department of Defense (DOD) along with other agencies (i.e., InterNIC) support standard documentation to categorize which ports are used for specific communications. Many vendors have accepted agreements to create software for similar purposes to all communicate on the same port (i.e., web browser creators such as "Firefox", "Chrome" and "Internet Explorer" all use ports 80 and 443 for default website viewing). Other ports are also standardized for other uses which may periodically move to other ports. Since there are 65,535 ports, many are not identified for any particular use. Any port can be utilized at any time for any transmission type without any updates to any international standard documents. Due to the different elements involved in the use of different ports, there are terms which are used to describe the port categories along with their respective numbers as in the following:

Port Range	Category
1-1023	Well-known
49152-65535	Dynamic
1024-49151	Registered

Although specific ports are associated with particular functions or software, it is possible to reconfigure software to utilize other ports. For example, "Telnet" uses port 23 while e-mail (SMTP) uses port 25. It is possible to configure telnet to test an e-mail server by making telnet use port 25. The process for testing an e-mail server is beyond the scope of this book, but it required mention for those who desire network certification. Often time on certification examinations, it is required to identify some specific ports and protocols within the "Well-known (Also called "Commonly Used")" or commonly used range. The table below displays many of the ports often manipulated in troubleshooting and or normally assessed on certification examinations:

Port	Protocol
20, 21	File Transfer Protocol (FTP)
23	Telnet
25	Simple Mail Transfer Protocol (SMTP)
53	Domain Name Server (DNS)
67, 68	Dynamic Host Configuration Protocol (DHCP)
69	Trivial File Transfer Protocol (TFTP)
80	HyperText Transfer Protocol (HTTP)
110	Post Office Protocol (POP3)
143	Internet Message Access Protocol (IMAP4)
443	HTTP with Secure Sockets Layer (SSL)
3389	Remote Desktop (RDP)

Nodes, Clients, Identities and Character-Types:

Depending on which protocol or software is used on a network, devices can be identified many different ways. The following methods are ways in which network devices display their existence as well as what can be used for communications between devices (Note: Regardless of the naming convention, many characters are not compatible with many names such as "spaces" between characters and some special symbols such as " \ " or " * "):

- **Hostname** = Using Alpha-Numeric characters (A-Z and 0-9). Examples would be "PC_17", "Dad_Computer", "Room_012" etc. This type of name is totally arbitrary and can be changed. A simple view of a hostname can be displayed on Windows systems by typing in "hostname" and pressing "enter" when using a CLI.
- **IP Address (Decimal)** = Characters are numeric (0-9) and are arranged in four sections separated by decimals (.) called "Octets". In addition, the primary numbers used in IPv4 networks are between 0 and 255 in each section. Examples are "192.168.1.10" or "169.254.101.20". IP address arrangements appear in many network-related settings on computers, cell phones, televisions, etc. This type of identity can randomly change depending on how the network interface is configured. A simple view of an IP address can be displayed on Windows systems by typing in "ipconfig" and pressing "enter" when using a CLI.
- **Mac Address (Hexadecimal)** = Also called a "Physical Address" and uses a limited arrangement of Alpha-Numeric characters including only 0-9 and A-F (There are other hexadecimal character combinations but the ones listed are used in network technology). Usually arranged in three groups of four characters separated by decimals or six groups of two characters separated by hyphens (-). Examples would be A9-6F-CE-AA-87-99. The mac-address is actually encoded in the network interface of a device. It is globally unique and more like a network device's "fingerprint". This identity is configured to be permanent and can only be changed by persons with higher levels of electronics, programming or cyber-security experience. A view of a devices physical address can be displayed on Windows systems by typing in "ipconfig /all" and pressing "enter" when using a CLI.
- **Binary** = Binary characters are the foundation of computer and software technology. These characters are represented with either a "0" or a "1". Combinations of binary characters cause actions in software, hardware and identify devices. Often with programming, the two options for bits have specific meanings as in the following:
  - o   0 = off, no or false.
  - o   1 = on, yes or true.

- Total numbers of combined characters have meaning in elements of instruction, storage and/or speed. Specific well-known combinations have the following names:
    - **Bit** = Single character as in "0" or "1".
    - **Nibble** = Four bits as in "0000" or "1111" or "0101".
    - **Byte** (Sometimes called an "Octet") = Eight bits, or two nibbles as in "11110000".

Chapter 4
Character Conversion Tables

Character Conversion Tables:

Many devices with one ID type must communicate with totally different device ID types. For this to occur, there is the need to convert between identities. For example, some situations require a binary identity to be displayed in decimal format. To understand this process, it is necessary to learn how to convert between the three following identities; decimal, binary and hexadecimal. A table which will be used a lot in this text is displayed below:

Network Related Numbers Conversion		
Decimal	Hexadecimal	Binary
0	0	0000
1	1	0001
2	2	0010
3	3	0011
4	4	0100
5	5	0101
6	6	0110
7	7	0111
8	8	1000
9	9	1001
10	A	1010
11	B	1011
12	C	1100
13	D	1101
14	E	1110
15	F	1111

There are many ways to convert numbers mathematically. When taking many certification examinations, calculators are not allowed and processing questions concerning math may result in a great loss of time (Most certification examinations have a specific time limit for completion). It is important to utilize a method which will render quicker results without the need for duplicated writing. In order to accomplish this goal, I (The writer) have created a "pointing table" which can expedite the process of number conversion as well as other related processes required in network technology and certifications. The writer has created a number of methods and tables which can assist the learning of conversions. One of the tables used is the "Decimal to Binary Conversions Table" displayed below:

Decimal to Binary Conversions

128	64	32	16	8	4	2	1

- **Formula Legend:**
  1. **N1** = Original number.
  2. **R#** = Resultant number.

With the table above, it is possible to translate decimal numbers to binary and the reverse. No higher order math is necessary. Simply place numbers into the "value spaces" and either add or subtract depending on the desired operation. Using the table above, perform the following:

- **Convert the decimal number "3" into a binary value. Here is the overview:**
  1) Moving "left to right" indicate a binary "1" for any spot which can be subtracted from N1.
  2) Moving "left to right" indicate a binary "0" for any spot which cannot be subtracted from N1.
  3) When a number can be subtracted, do so and continue using the result (R#)

Let's work the problem:
- Step 1 = Left to right, find the value spot which can be SUBTRACTED FROM "3" (N1).
  1. The value spot "128" cannot be subtracted from "3".
     - Place a "0" in the binary row beneath the value spot.
     - Continue moving to the right.
  2. The value spot "64" cannot be subtracted from "3".
     - Place a "0" in the binary row beneath the value spot.
     - Continue moving to the right.
  3. The value spot "32" cannot be subtracted from "3".
     - Place a "0" in the binary row beneath the value spot.
     - Continue moving to the right.
  4. The value spot "16" cannot be subtracted from "3".
     - Place a "0" in the binary row beneath the value spot.
     - Continue moving to the right.
  5. The value spot "8" cannot be subtracted from "3".

➤ Place a "0" in the binary row. Continue moving to the right.

6. The value spot "4" cannot be subtracted from "3".
   ➤ Place a "0" in the binary row beneath the value spot.
   ➤ Continue moving to the right.

7. The value spot "2" CAN be subtracted from "3".
   ➤ Subtract the value spot (2) from the original number "3".
   ➤ We now using the remainder of "1" as the number we are evaluating.
      ❖ We call this "R1" (The digit changes based on what was left after subtracting the found number from N1).
   ➤ Place a "1" in the binary row beneath the value spot.
   ➤ Continue moving to the right.

8. The value spot "1" can be subtracted from "1" (R1).
   ➤ Subtract the number in the value spot (1) from the result number "1"
   ➤ We now using the remainder of "0" as the number we are evaluating.
      ❖ We call this "R2" (The digit changes based on changing resultants).
   ➤ Place a "1" in the binary row beneath the value spot. The results will look like table below:

Decimal to Binary Conversions							
128	64	32	16	8	4	2	1
0	0	0	0	0	0	1	1
X	X	X	X	X	X	(-2)	(0)

9. Going from left to right, add up all the value spot numbers which have a "1" beneath them (2 + 1 = 3).
10. The binary equivalent of the decimal number "3" = 00000011.
    ➤ Some books drop the zeros before the first 1 which makes the number display as "11". Don't be fooled. Always keep the zeros in mind!

Let's try another: **Find the binary version of the decimal number 40.**
Remember the steps:

- Moving "left to right" indicate a binary "1" for any spot which can be subtracted from N1.
- Moving "left to right" indicate a binary "0" for any spot which cannot be subtracted from N1.
- When a number can be subtracted, do so and continue using the result (R#). In this case "N1" = "40"
  - Step 1 = Left to right, find the value spot which can be SUBTRACTED FROM "40" (N1).
    1. The value spot "128" cannot be subtracted from "40".
       - Place a "0" in the binary row beneath the value spot.
       - Continue moving to the right.
    2. The value spot "64" cannot be subtracted from "40".
       - Place a "0" in the binary row beneath the value spot.
       - Continue moving to the right.
    3. The value spot "32" CAN be subtracted from "40".
       - Subtract the number in the value spot (32) from the original number "40" (N1) leaving the first result of 8 (R1).
       - We are now using "8" as the number we are evaluating.
         - ❖ We call this "R1" (The digit changes based on changing resultants).
         - ❖ Continue moving to the right.
    4. The value spot "16" cannot be subtracted from "8".
       - Place a "0" in the binary row beneath the value spot.
       - Continue moving to the right.
    5. The value spot "8" CAN be subtracted from "8".
       - Subtract the number in the value spot (8) from the first result number "8" (R1) leaving the second result of 0 (R2).
       - We are now using "0" as the number we are evaluating.
         - ❖ We call this "R2" (The digit changes based on changing resultants).
       - Continue moving to the right.
    6. The value spot "4" cannot be subtracted from "0".
       - Place a "0" in the binary row beneath the value spot.
       - Continue moving to the right.
    7. The value spot "2" cannot be subtracted from "0".
       - Place a "0" in the binary row beneath the value spot.
       - Continue moving to the right.
    8. The value spot "2" cannot be subtracted from "0".

> Place a "0" in the binary row beneath the value spot.
9. Going from left to right, add up all the value spot numbers which have a "1" beneath them (32 + 8 = 4).

Decimal to Binary Conversions							
128	64	32	16	8	4	2	1
0	0	1	0	1	0	0	0
X	X	(-8)	X	(-0)	X	X	X

10. The binary equivalent of the decimal number "40" = 00101000.
> Some books drop the zeros before the first 1 which makes the number display as "101000". Don't be fooled. Always keep the zeros in mind.

Try a few of the numbers below on your own. Convert the following decimal numbers into binary:

1. 129 = Answer 10000001
2. 70 = Answer 01000110
3. 20 = Answer 00010100
4. 10 = Answer 00001010
5. 250 = Answer 11111010

How to Convert "Hexadecimal" to "Binary"

The characters include both reading letters and decimal numbers limited to "0 thru 9" and "A – F". Computers cannot process double-characters such as the number "13" or "10". In order to process double digit numbers for network technology (Or numbers higher than the decimal number "9") a letter was selected to represent certain numbers which have two digits. The following table show the numbers which are represented by each hexadecimal character:

Hex	Represents		
1	1		
2	2		
3	3		
4	4	A	10
5	5	B	11
6	6	C	12
7	7	D	13
8	8	E	14
9	9	F	15

Remember, computers only show letter and number characters so humans can understand the message. Router and Switches have to use binary numbers. With hexadecimal numbers, each character is actually a representation of a collection of binary characters ("0's" or "1's"). Each character always represents four "bits" **(Called a "Nibble"). Understanding that a MAC has 12 hexadecimal characters, multiplying each character by "four bits" will render a total number of 128 bits**. These bits are what are used by computer hardware and software for functions. The hexadecimal readout is only so humans can better differentiate between different MACS. In the field of network technology, it is necessary to understand how binary collections create specific MAC addresses. To provide this function the following "Hex to Binary" table is used:

Hex to Binary Conversions								
A	8	4	2	1	8	4	2	1
B								
C								

Notice that the table is similar to the "Decimal to Binary" scale in which it has eight "value spaces" and it has three levels. The following are the functions of each level:

- **A-Level (Value Areas)** = Indicates 8,4,2,1-8,4,2,1
- **B-Level (Yes/No Area)** = Indicates if can be subtracted from hexadecimal character.
- **C-Level (Hex Character)** = Specific character being evaluated.

Using the table, it is possible to convert between hexadecimal characters and their associated "nibbles" or binary equivalence. Using the table and a process, we can carry out the conversion using the following the steps:
1. Locate a full 12-character MAC address.
2. Isolate the first set of Hex characters (Separated by " : " or " . ").
3. Locate the "Left-most" hex character in and place in "C=Left" of the conversion table.
4. Locate the "Right-most" hex character in and place in "C=Right" of the conversion table.
5. Subtract all "A-Row" numbers from the "C-Row" numbers from left to right.
6. All numbers you cannot subtract, record as a binary "0" in the "B-Row".

7. All numbers you can subtract, record as a binary "1" in the B-Row and retain remainder for next subtraction.
8. Continue until you have two complete "Nibbles" on the "B-Row".

Take the following example: Given the MAC address of 23-3C-DD-AB-FE-72, what is the binary version of the 2nd character set? Let's work the problem:
- 2nd character set = "3C"
- Place the characters on the conversion chart as in the following (Remember to convert "Letters" into corresponding "Numbers"):

	Hex to Binary Conversions							
A	8	4	2	1	8	4	2	1
B								
C	Left = 3				Right = C (12)			

- Begin the subtraction process on the "Left-Side" with the character "3":
  1. Ask the question "Is this a LETTER or a NUMBER?".
     ➤ If character is a LETTER use conversion chart to change to correlated number and go to step #2.

Hex	Represents
A	10
B	11
C	12
D	13
E	14
F	15

     ➤ If character is a NUMBER, continue to step #2.
  2. Can you subtract 8 from 3 = No (Which is "0" in binary).
     ➤ Place a "0" in the "8-B" slot.
     ➤ Continue to next "A-Row" number.
  3. Can you subtract 4 from 3 = No (Which is "0" in binary).
     ➤ Place a "0" in the "4-B" slot.
     ➤ Continue to next "A-Row" number.

4. Can you subtract 2 from 3 = Yes (Which is "1" in binary).
   ➤ Place a "1" in the "2-B" slot.
   ➤ What remains of the original number?
      o 3 – 2 = 1 (In decimal).
      o Now use "1" as the number in the "C" slot.
   ➤ Continue to next "A-Row" number.
5. Can you subtract 1 from 1 = Yes (Which is "1" in binary).
   ➤ Place a "1" in the "1-B" slot.
   ➤ What remains of the original number?
      o 0 (In decimal).

- All bits on the "Left Side" have been created resulting in "0011" which is the "nibble" for the hexadecimal character "3". Below:

Hex to Binary Conversions								
A	8	4	2	1	8	4	2	1
B	0	0	1	1				
C	Left = 3				Right = C (12)			

- Now continue to do the same for the "Right Side" which has the character "C".

1. Ask the question "Is this a LETTER or a NUMBER?".
   ➤ If character is a LETTER use conversion chart to change to correlated number and go to step #2.
      o The character "C" equals the decimal number "12". Insert "12" into the "C-Right" box and subtract all "B-Row" numbers from "12".

Hex Represents	
A	10
B	11
C	12
D	13
E	14
F	15

   ➤ If character is a NUMBER, continue to step #2.

2. Can you subtract 8 from 12 = Yes (Which is "1" in binary).
   ➤ Place a "1" in the "8-B" slot.
   ➤ What remains of the original number?
     ○ 12 – 8 = 4 (In decimal).
     ○ Now use "4" as the number in the "C" slot.
   ➤ Continue to next "A-Row" number.
3. Can you subtract 4 from 4 = Yes (Which is "1" in binary).
   ➤ Place a "1" in the "4-B" slot.
   ➤ What remains of the original number?
     ○ 4 – 4 = 0 (In decimal).
     ○ Now use "0" as the number in the "C" slot.
   ➤ Place a "0" in the "4-B" slot.
   ➤ Continue to next "A-Row" number.
4. Can you subtract 2 from 0 = No (Which is "0" in binary).
   ➤ Place a "0" in the "2-B" slot.
   ➤ Continue to next "A-Row" number.
5. Can you subtract 1 from 0 = No (Which is "0" in binary).

- All bits on the "Right Side" have been created resulting in "1100" which is the "nibble" for the hexadecimal character "C". The results appear as follows:

Hex to Binary Conversions							
A	8	4	2	1	8	4	2	1
B	0	0	1	1	1	1	0	0
C	Left = 3				Right = C (12)			

- This give us the total answer that the hexadecimal combination "3C" = "00111100" in binary! Outstanding!!! Let's try another!

Take the following example: Given the MAC address of 23-3C-DD-AB-FE-72, what is the binary version of the 4th character set? Let's work the problem:
- 4th character set = "AB"
- Place the characters on the conversion chart as in the following (Remember to convert "Letters" into corresponding "Numbers"):

Hex to Binary Conversions								
A	8	4	2	1	8	4	2	1
B								
C	Left = A (10)				Right = B (11)			

- Begin the subtraction process on the "Left-Side" with the character "A":
  1. Ask the question "Is this a LETTER or a NUMBER?".
     - We can see that the letter "A" has a decimal value of "10". Now continue to step #2.

Hex	Represents
A	10
B	11
C	12
D	13
E	14
F	15

  2. Can you subtract 8 from 10 = Yes (Which is "1" in binary).
     - Place a "1" in the "8-B" slot.
     - What remains of the original number?
       - 10 – 8 = 2 (In decimal).
       - Now use "2" as the number in the "C" slot.
     - Continue to next "A-Row" number.
  3. Can you subtract 4 from 2 = No (Which is "0" in binary).
     - Place a "0" in the "4-B" slot.
     - Continue to next "A-Row" number.
  4. Can you subtract 2 from 2 = Yes (Which is "1" in binary).
     - Place a "1" in the "2-B" slot.
     - What remains of the original number?
       - 2 – 2 = 0 (In decimal).
       - Now use "0" as the number in the "C" slot.
     - Continue to next "A-Row" number.

5. Can you subtract 1 from 0 = No (Which is "1" in binary).
   ➤ Place a "0" in the "1-B" slot.

- All bits on the "Left Side" have been created resulting in "1010" which is the "nibble" for the hexadecimal character "A" as in below:

Hex to Binary Conversions								
A	8	4	2	1	8	4	2	1
B	1	0	1	0				
C	Left = A (10)				Right = B (11)			

- Now continue to do the same for the "Right Side" which has the character "B".
   1. Ask the question "Is this a LETTER or a NUMBER?".
      ➤ If character is a LETTER use conversion chart to change to correlated number and go to step #2.
         o The character "B" equals the decimal number "11". Insert "11" into the "C-Right" box and subtract all "B-Row" numbers from "11".

Hex	Represents
A	10
B	11
C	12
D	13
E	14
F	15

   2. Can you subtract 8 from 11 = Yes (Which is "1" in binary).
      ➤ Place a "1" in the "8-B" slot.
      ➤ What remains of the original number?
         o 11 – 8 = 3 (In decimal).
         o Now use "3" as the number in the "C" slot.
      ➤ Continue to next "A-Row" number.
   3. Can you subtract 4 from 3 = No (Which is "0" in binary).
      ➤ Place a "0" in the "4-B" slot.

> Continue to next "A-Row" number.

4. Can you subtract 2 from 3 = Yes (Which is "1" in binary).
   > Place a "1" in the "2-B" slot.
   > What remains of the original number?
     o 3 − 2 = 1 (In decimal).
     o Now use "1" as the number in the "C" slot.
   > Continue to next "A-Row" number.

5. Can you subtract 1 from 1 = Yes (Which is "1" in binary).
   > Place a "1" in the "1-B" slot.
   > What remains of the original number?
     o 1 − 1 = 0 (In decimal).

6. All bits on the "Right Side" have been created resulting in "1011" which is the "nibble" for the hexadecimal character "B". The results appear as follows:

Hex to Binary Conversions							
A	8	4	2	1	8	4	2	1
B	1	0	1	0	1	0	1	1
C	Left = A (10)				Right = B (11)			

- This give us the total answer that the hexadecimal combination "AB" = "10101011" in binary! Make up a few of your own and practice!

Because a MAC is unique and does not change, there is no major need to configure them (Unless creating more secure networks using IP version 6). In the field of cisco technology, however, there are requirements of understanding the construction of a MAC address. Although the hexadecimal characters are in groups of two, there are actually two major sections of a MAC address. They are identified as the "First Six" and the "Last Six" characters as follows:

- **CC:CC:CC:MM:MM:MM**
- **CC-CC-CC-MM-MM-MM**

  o **First Six Characters (Represented by "CC")** = Represent the company or business which originally created the network interface such as "Dell", "IBM", etc. Each company which manufactures network interfaces are issued this unique number from Arpanet and the

Department of Defense for security reasons. The MAC address of a device is often used to track down cyber criminals. All companies which create network interfaces keep records of all of them and where the card was installed or sold. You can insert the first six characters in an internet search and locate which company originally created or sold the network interface.

o **Last Six Characters (Represented by "MM")** = Identify the special make, model or creation date of the network interface. Often times, groups of the characters indicate that the model has special features such as "Wake on LAN" which would allow a computer to be turned on as long as it is connected to a network. Some high-end network interfaces are actually "mini-computers" which allow complete control of an entire computer even when the computer's power state is turned off.

Chapter 5
IP Addressing Versions and Concepts

IP Addressing Versions and Concepts:

Regardless of the type of software used or the type of network devices they all require identity information. We discussed the following identities in the section "Nodes, Clients and Identities". Different protocols use many different identities for communication but for our discussions we will primarily discuss "IP Addresses". The following areas will be the focus of the discussion of this book concerning IP addresses:

- **IP Version 4** = One of the primary standards established by ARPANET for network identities on the internet. Although worldwide organizations formally established it in the mid-1980's, IPv4 routes much Internet traffic today and will more than likely exist for quite some time. Elements which allow IPv4's continued existence is in the elements that it is a widely used protocol in data communication and allows compatibility across a number of different network types. Multiple types of network devices support IPv4 and there are many features such as "Dynamic Host Configuration Protocol", "Vender Class" and many other utilities. IPv4 is a connectionless protocol which means that the source and destination does not have a dedicated connection but uses intermediary devices to transmit data in a "Relay-Race" fashion". It provides the logical connection between network devices by providing identification for each device. Due to this configuration, there is a possibility of failed delivery or even duplicated data being sent. Although the protocol has errors inherent in its composition, higher level protocols protect against errors. IPv4 uses a 32-bit (four-byte) method allowing for a total of 2^32 addresses (just over 4 billion addresses). The addresses are converted from binary to decimal when displayed for better understanding for humans. Because of the demand of the growing Internet, the available numbers of remaining addresses were nearing exhaustion anticipated between 2004 and 2011. The problem concerning "lack of available network addresses for the internet" was foreseen many years prior which gave rise to other methods of network addressing for the internet.

- **IP Version 6** = Internet Protocol version 6 (IPv6) is the version of the Internet Protocol (IP) initiated for use near the year 2011 which provides an identification for servers, routers and network devices system across the Internet. IPv6 was developed by the Internet Engineering Task Force (IETF) to address the foreseen exhaustion of available of IPv4 addresses. IPv6 uses a 128-bit address which provides for 2^28 which is a number so large it is said to be an "Undecillion". IPv6 addresses are represented as eight groups of four "Hextets" or "Hexwords" separated by colons such as in the example; "2001:1234:abcd:9944:c675:cf00:36bb:94ee". The example given in the previous sentence is called "uncompressed" although many times, the full address can be compressed by eliminating groups of zeros.

- **Classfull IP addressing** = Primary method used on the Internet from 1981 to about early 1990's. Using the Classfull method, address spaces are divided into five address classes of "A, B and C" with two more of "D" which is for "multicasting" and "E" reserved for military and experimental purposes. Below is an example of Classfull IP addressing:

Traditional Classfull IP Address Standards			
Class	Leading Octet	Subnet Mask	Maximum Hosts
A	0-127	255.0.0.0	16,777,214
B	128 - 191	255.255.0.0	65,534
C	192 - 223	255.255.255.0	254
D	224 - 239	Multicast	NA
E	240 - 247	Military Use	NA

Notes:
1) The "Leading Octet Ranges" display mathematical derivatives including reserved octets.
2) "Maximum Hosts" displays "Usable" hosts and not the pure mathematical derivatives.

- **Classless IP Addressing** = Due to the growth of the internet, there was a need to extend the range of available addressing. IPv6 is a method but the primary restriction to it is that older IPv4 devices could not communicate using IPv6. A solution to the decreasing number of available IPv4 addresses was produced with the implementation of CIDR and VLSM:
  1. **Classless Internet Domain Routing (CIDR)** = When networks were developed, traffic was routed based on matching Classfull IP Classes (i.e., "A", "B", "C", etc.) with a specific subnet mask ("255.0.0.0", "255.255.0.0" or "255.255.255.0"). Due to the increase in the number of devices, classfull IP addressing could not support the number of routes on the internet. IPv6 was created, but IPv4 will not understand routing from IPv6. Due to this challenge, programmers began to re-compile router and switch operating systems to utilize the "binary" form of numbers as opposed to the traditional method of "decimal" utilization. Because of this enhancement, subnet masks can include the following new octets: 128, 192, 224, 240, 248, 252, and 254. These new octets are combined with traditional IP addresses as in the examples below:

CIDR Examples	
Host IP	**Subnet Mask**
204.16.10.54	255.255.255.128
199.240.78.95	255.255.240.0
224.16.76.81	255.255.255.192

Netmask Conversions		
Binary	Octet	CIDR
10000000	128	/25
11000000	192	/26
11100000	224	/27
11110000	240	/28
11111000	248	/29
11111100	252	/30
11111110	254	/31
11111111	255	NA (Or /32)
Assumes 1st three octets of "255.255.255.x"		

> Although decimal numbers are displayed, the arrangement of the "Binary "0's" and "1's" dictate network parameters such as:
>   ❖ Number of networks
>   ❖ Number of hosts
>   ❖ Paths between networks

2. **Variable Length Subnet Masks (VLSM)** = Paralleling the utilization of CIDR, the method of documenting IP configurations has also evolved. As opposed to using decimal numbers, the amount of "1's" in "binary" are added up and a decimal number is used to reflect the total written at the end of an IP address after a "/" character (Often called a "forward slash"). Take the following for example:
   > Traditional subnet mask = 255.255.255.128
      ❖ Binary format 11111111.11111111.11111111.10000000
      ❖ Count number of binary "1's" = 8+8+8+1 = 25 total.
      ❖ VLSM documentation = /25

3. **Reserved Addresses** = When using IPv4, IPv6 or CIDR, specific types of IP addresses have special uses. We often call these addresses "Reserved" or "Special Use". Regardless of their use, they both have one common element. Reserved IP addresses are not to be used on devices directly connected to the internet (On the Department of Defense backbone). If reserved IP addresses are used on devices

which are directly connected to the internet backbone, the situation will result in the device not communication or a conflict with other devices on the internet. The following are some of the "reserved" addresses:

- **169.254.X.Y** = Network systems will self-assign an address within in this range if a DHCP server cannot be contacted.
- **192.168.X.Y** = Often used for private networks or training purposes.
- **127.0.0.1** = This is called the "loopback" and "localhost" address. This address is used as a utility to ascertain if a network devices interface can be contacted by the rest of the network. The loopback is often used if the network devices IP address is hidden. Using a "ping" command, a technician can perform the following to test if the network device he or she is working on can be contacted by other devices.
- Some other reserved IP address appear in the chart below:

Reserved/Special Use IP Addresses
10.0.0.0 – 10.255.255.255
172.16.0.0 – 172.31.255.255
192.168.0.0 – 192.168.255.255
127.0.0.1 - 127.255.255.254

IP Address Sections:

Based on the communication requirements on a network, various methods of node identification can be used (As in the prior mentioned methods of "hostname", "physical address" and/or "IP address", etc.). When using IP addresses, specific sections of an address have terms which are used to describe their purpose.

- **Network Address/ID** = The section of an IP address which all nodes on a section of a network have in common. Often times, it is the leading numbers on an IP address leading from left to right. An example would be 209.15.X.Y subnet mask of 255.255.0.0. The first two octets identify the network address (Traditionally, the section of the subnet mask will give an idea of the network address because whichever octet section used by the network address ID will reflect the same number of "255's" in the subnet mask.

1. Think of it like a "last name" on a family. There could be multiple people in a family. Such as the "Smith" family. All of the people in the family could be referred to as "the Smith" family. A network or network section uses the network address and it is common on all computers such as in the "Branch Office" network.

- **Host ID/node ID** = Section of an IP address which is unique for individual systems. This would be like the "first name" of all the people in the "Smith" family. There could be "Bob Smith", "Sam Smith" and "Sally Smith". In reference to a network, think of the following computers:
    1. 172.16.10.10 = Part of the "172.16.10" network but the host ID is "10".
    2. 172.16.10.15 = Part of the "172.16.10" network but the host ID is "15".
    3. 172.16.10.20 = Part of the "172.16.10" network but the host ID is "20".

Chapter 6
Cisco IOS Licensing

Cisco IOS Licensing (As of OS Code 15.0):

Originally, when an operating system was installed, it only had the features native to that version. For example, some versions of the Cisco IOS would not perform DHCP functions. If you desired a router to perform DHCP, you had to replace the operating system with a newer version. As time progressed, more recent operating systems would come with every function associated with the models of routers on which it could be installed. Recently, Cisco instituted a licensing model in which specific options are disabled unless the software is "activated". Once activated, the owner of the operating system can then "unlock" the desired features. In order to get access to a Cisco IOS you will have to use a PAK (Product Authorization Key). This is gained from Cisco when you provide them two pieces of information about your router. You will need the router's "UDI (Unique Device Identifier)" and the "PID (Product ID)".

The default Cisco IOS comes in what is called the "IP Base" license which essentially allows the installation and full use of all features for about 60 days. If a different IOS is needed for a router, it can be purchased from Cisco or any of Cisco's authorized resellers. The scope of this book does not include the full depth of IOS licensing, but the following are some commands often used in the process:

- **Commands for displaying licensing:**
  - Sh ver
  - Show license udi (Unique Device Identifier = Classifies a Part)
  - Show license all
  - Show license feature

- **Command for installing/activating license:**
  - License install flash:<NameOfLicense>.lic

- **Installing evaluation packages:**
  - (Config)# license boot module <ModelofRouter> technology-package <NameOfPackage> (This is all one line.)

You must accept the license agreement afterwards and then reboot the router for the license to be activated.

- **Backing up the license:**
  - DMZ_Router#License save flash:CIOSv1.lic

Most of these commands require reboot after installations of the IOS. There are many more functions availed and/or required in installing, modifying and updating the Cisco IOS. As mentioned before, the additional features are beyond the scope and purpose of this book.

Chapter 7
Traditional Network Devices

Traditional Network Devices:

Networks today include many different devices supplying various functions such as shared files, live video, e-mail and many other functions. Regardless of the type, speed and expanse of the network, there are a few devices which are traditionally part of all networks. The following are some devices typical on contemporary networks:

- **Hubs** = Once the primary device which connected computers together into what is referred to as a "network". Due to their time of existence, hubs range from older 10BaseT to higher speed networks. There are even hubs which have BNC connectors to allow the connection to coaxial based networks. In addition to connecting network devices, they also have the purpose of extending the length of sections of a network to allow the coverage of a larger distance between computer systems. In the development of hubs, simple technologies were used to support the priority of connecting computers. Hubs separate PDU's by alternating when individual computers would have the opportunity to transmit via using CSMA/CD (Carrier Sense Multiple Access-Collision Detection). Using CSMA/CD, nodes on a network would all transmit as needed. If any PDU's enter the hub simultaneously (Called a "Collision), the hub generates a "jam signal" to all ports which terminates all communications and requires all computers connected to the hub to pause all transmissions for a random amount of time (In milliseconds). This results in the following considerations when connecting network devices to a Hub:
  1. **Single PDU processing** = A hub allows only a single PDU to pass thru it at any given time. Whichever device has the smaller time for its pause, would be allowed to transmit its data first, followed by the device with the next shortest pause interval.
  2. **Divided bandwidth** = The maximum speed of a hub is related to the number of devices to which it is connected. Take the following for example.
     - 10 Port Hub rated at 10Mbps:
       - Connect 5 devices = Bandwidth is reduced to 2Mbps per connection.
       - Connect 10 devices = Bandwidth is reduced to 1Mbps per connection.
  3. **Proximity Access** = Standard hubs have no network circuitry other then what supports passing PDU's. This limitation results in requiring that there is always easy access to a switch in order

to address any problems it may experience. In addition, there are no options for remote management or security features.

> The size of networks were extremely small compared to today's standards (In the 1990's, there might be only 25 computers in a 15-story dormitory holding 450 students). Today, that same dormitory might have a computer in every students' room. Hubs are now largely obsolete except for SOHO installations (Small Office-Home Office).

- **SOHO-Switch** = A SOHO (Small Office-Home Office) switch has all of the characteristics of a Hub but eliminates two disadvantaged possessed by hubs:
    1. A switch will not divide bandwidth. If the hub is rated at 10Mbps, all ports will accept communications at that speed.
    2. Hubs allow multiple lines of communications between devices to occur simultaneously.

- **Corporate Switch** = Serving as the primary "distribution" node for a network, Switches are essential in the functioning of a major network. Corporate level Switches (Also called a Layer 2 Device) allow communication between thousands of systems simultaneously. Normally, switches exist on individual floors of buildings and continue to connect to one another in series. There is at least one switch which connects between all the switches and the single router for the building which in turns connect to the ISP (Internet Service Provider). The following are some of the characteristic of Corporate level switches:
    1. **Work out the box** = Switches will begin to route PDU's immediately. Plugging in most switches will allow electricity to flow and circuitry to pass packets between devices. In addition, some switches have PoE (Power over Ethernet). PoE indicates that the switch can transmit electricity over at least two of the wires in the category cable in order to supply power to devices connected to the cable such as wireless access points and Voice Over Internet Protocol telephone systems (VoIP).
    2. **Remote Management** = A helpful feature of corporate switches is the ability to control the device via both a standard management protocol called "Telnet" and support control features using an internet browser-based "WebUI" (Web User Interface). This is a helpful feature because as long as the switch is powered on and has an IP address which can be contacted, there is no need to be in the same physical location

of the switch. Essentially, the network administrator can reach the device from anywhere in the world that has internet access.

3. **Configuration** = Although switches operate as soon as they have electricity, there are dozens of features available. Using a "corporate level" switch without customizing the device is essentially wasting thousands of dollars (Most corporate level switches cost above $3,000.00 each). The following are some of the aspects or functions available on corporate switches:

> **Interface and Port types** = Normally there are about three types of interfaces available on switches. Any of which can be used to connect, configure or modify a switch. Many ports can have a username and password associated to prohibit unauthorized access or configuration of the switch. In addition, all of these passwords can be "Encrypted" (Process of making text and message illegible for unauthorized users). In addition to protecting the switch from users, many Switch and Router operating systems allow placing credentials on the actual device so it can validate its identity to other Switches, Routers and network devices. Below are some of the ports normally on switches:

❖ **Console Port** = Primarily used to configure a switch but can also be used to upload files such as configurations and operating systems. Traditionally, this port has a "light blue" color to associate it with the console cable used to configure a router. There is another cable which mimics the design of a console cable called an "Aux" cable which can also be connected to this port.

❖ **Auxiliary Port (Aux)** = This port is a "legacy" connection used as a backup connection to the router in the event the device is failing. In addition, it can often be connected to a modem to temporally route traffic if the primary network connections were to fail. The port normally has a "black" color associating it with a console cable which is also "black".

❖ **Ethernet-based ports** = These ports are used to connect network devices such as routers, computers, telephones, cameras, other switches, etc. The traffic that the switch processes travels along these ports. Depending on the age and cost of the switch, they can vary in speed.

Some of the speeds available at the time of writing this book are 10Mbps, 100Mbps, 1000Mbps (Often called "Gigabit Ethernet") and also 10-GigE (10,000 Mbps). The ports are often associated with the color "yellow".

❖ **Fiber Ports** = These ports support the connection of a fine material wire which allows the transmission of light from emitters on either end. Fiber cable is often used for extremely long distances between network devices such as building and cities. Fiber optic cable is also very fast with its slowest speed being 1000Mbps ("Gigabit Ethernet"). Fiber is also more stable because it is not susceptible to various types of interference such as EMI (Electric Magnetic Interference) or RFI (Radio Frequency Interference).

➢ **Backup and restore of configurations and operating systems** = It often takes weeks to setup and configure a network device. After a device has all settings stable, it is possible to save the configurations to a TFTP server (Trivial File Transfer Protocol). In this way, if the original switch is replaced, the settings can be moved to the replacement device reducing the time a network is offline. In addition, the entire operating system on a device can also be backed-up or restored to a replacement device.

➢ **Setup Mode (System Configuration Dialog)** = Upon startup of a Switch or Router, if it has no configurations, the device will initiate the startup of a list of questions in which a technician could supply answers to which the device will store as configurations. The disadvantage is that the settings which might be needed may not be requested in the "Setup mode" question lists. Most technicians do not utilize "setup-mode".

➢ **User Login** = Corporate switches provide various levels of access. Each level result in a greater ability to configure, manage and evaluate the condition of a switch. There are 3 (Sometimes listed as 4) levels of access available on Switches and Routers. Each level denotes what activities can be performed on the network device. The levels of users appear below with the associated prompt indicator:

❖ **(>) User Exec** = This mode allows the user to execute only the basic commands, such as those that show the system's status and pings.

❖ **(#) Privileged** = View the system configuration, restart the system, check clock time and other minor changes to device.

❖ **(config)# Global configuration** = Allows major changes to Switch or Router configuration security, traffic processing, protocols used and security features.

❖ **(config-router/if/dhcp/etc) # Specific Configuration** = Affects unique options, aspects, protocol, service or interface on a switch or router. The unique area represented in the prompt above is for "Dynamic Host Configuration".

❖ **Banners** = Supporting easy identification or location of switches and routers. The operating system allows a message to be displayed when attempting to login or access a switch. Banners also support legal requirements to post warnings of who is allowed to access a device and the punishment for unauthorized connections.

❖ **VLANS (Virtual Local Area Networks)** = Provides divisions between which devices on networks are allowed to communicate with one another. Essentially, the switch will "segment" or "organize" its ports into collections of which ones are allowed to exchange frames. This serves two purposes:

    1) **Bandwidth Congestion** = The individual ports in VLANs cannot communicate with ports in other VLANs. The result is that when one VLAN is highly congested with network traffic, the other VLANS are not affected at all. The process of traffic disabling traffic is called a "bottleneck".

    2) **Security** = Separating network devices causes different VLANs to be inaccessible on that particular switch. This will create challenges for anyone who uses one VLAN to attempt to compromise others.

➤ **VTP (Virtual Trunking Protocol)** = This protocol exists on routers and switches to allow rules of VLANs to be duplicated on other VLAN-enabled devices. When enabled, names and numbers of VLANs can be duplicated with only simple interactions with a network administrator. VTP results in the configuration of three different characters or functions on a network which incorporates VLAN technology and practices:

❖ **VTP Mode Server** = From this switch, it is possible to create, distribute and delete VLAN information.

❖ **VTP Domain** = Security boundary which allows different duplication of VLAN information to be transferred to participating switches. Switches in other VTP domains will not receive updates or changes.

❖ **VTP Mode Client** = Receive VLAN information from VTP server in charge of the VTP domain in which it resides. This switch will not allow any changes, addition or deletions to the VLAN domain in which it participates.

❖ **VTP Mode Transparent** = Indicates that the switch is physically connected to other switches which are in VTP domains. In transparent mode, VLAN frames will pass thru the switch but the switch will not participate in the domains of which it is aware.

➢ **STP (Spanning-Tree Protocol)** = STP assists in the routing of traffic by identifying pathways on networks. In addition, STP locates multiple connections to the same network location and eliminates duplicated paths. The protocols primary feature is to stop routing loops which occur when traffic constantly retraces it path on a network without reaching its destination. If the packets cannot find their destination, they would never leave the network. If packets cannot leave the network, the result would be "congestion" which is a network version of a "traffic jam". After enough packets are randomly circling the network, other traffic would be prevented from reaching their destinations.

• **Routers** = Serving as the primary "Connection" node between building and separated networks. Routers (Also called a Layer 3 Device) allow communication between the different buildings and networks comprising the internet. Normally, each building has at least a single router which is connected to the "Core Switch" of a building on side and the Internet

Service Provider (ISP) on the other. Essentially, routers have features similar to Switches such as telnet, ports, remote management, Backups, Command Line Interface (CLI), etc plus additional features. The following are some of the characteristic of Routers:

1. **Must be configured to Pass Data/Traffic** = Routers have absolutely no settings on them when they are brand new. They pass any traffic upon turning them on. Every route, pathway and access rule required on a router has to be manually initiated by a network technician. The command set used for routers is similar to those of a Switch with a few additional parameters.

2. **Routing Tables** = This is a list of how the router can move traffic thru and in between other networks.

Chapter 8
Setup and Configuration of Network Devices

Setup and Configuration of Network Devices

The bases for most network communications are established around interfaces, addressing and protocols. Prior to any of the aforementioned elements communicating network devices must be manually configured. While minor network devices (i.e., hubs and small home network technology) requires no interaction from a user other than turning it on, corporate-level network technology requires a skilled technician to initiate sessions, test bandwidth and troubleshoot data disconnects on a daily basis. The following paragraphs give an overview regarding the processes involved with configuring and connecting network devices.

- **Connection Methods** = There many methods of connecting Switches and Routers. The method chosen totally depends on the network technology involved and the background of the network technician. Below are some of the tools and software used by persons in the network technology field:
    1. **Console Cable (Rolled)** = A cable which often looks "Flat" is connected to a computers serial port (Often called a "Com" port) while the other end is inserted into a router or a switch. Because of network standards, the color of this type of cable is often "light blue" or "black" (Black cables attempt to identify the fact that these cables can also fit and be used in the "Auxiliary" port on a router or switch.

    2. **USB Console Cable** = This cable is similar to the rolled console cable in color and flatness but the ends (Terminators) on the cable have USB interfaces on one or both ends.

3. **IP-Based network** = When corporate-level (Not "Small Office Home Office (SOHO") routers and switches are first taken out of their boxes as "new" they have no settings which would allow them to communicate on a network. After a console cable has been used to configure options like passwords and IP address, a network device can be configured without being in physical proximity of the device. Essentially, if the device is connected to your cooperate network (i.e., LAN, MAN or WAN) or anywhere on the internet, a tech would be able to connect to the device using it's IP address combined with various network utilities and software.

Network Utilities (Software and Commands):

Working on networks often requires various tasks such as identification of devices, location of routes of travel and other elements common to communication networks. In our present day of technology, many operating systems and devices include applications and software-based tools to assist in network assessment and troubleshooting. Many of these tools require the familiarization with the use of the "CLI (Command Line Interface)". The following are commands which prove very useful when interacting or repairing network devices:

- **Hostname** = This command appears in Microsoft Operating Systems and Cisco Devices. Depending on the platform, it can display the alpha-numeric identity of a system and/or change the identity of the system.
- **Ipconfig** = Displays basic required network settings on Microsoft platforms. The command also has an optional modification of the command which will show a complete display of communication configurations. In order to use the enhanced features, additional words and characters must be appended to the command. The character which must

be added is often called a "Forward Slash" or a "switch". The character visually is represented by using "/".

    1. Available switches:
- **All** = Displays interfaces, protocols and settings.
- **Release** = Informs the DHCP server the client no longer requires an IP address.
- **Renew** = Requests an IP address from a DHCP server.

- **Ping** = Assesses the ability of one network device to contact another network device. Often used to assess if a computer can reach a printer or someplace on the internet. Much like other command line utilities, there are options available to manipulate the data reported by the "ping" command such as the following switches:
  1. **–t** = Continually attempt to find target IP until "cancel" command is executed (Ctrl+C).
  2. **–n** (Count) = Set number of times to attempt to contact target IP.
- **Pathping** = Displays the path and amount of message (Packet) loss occurring in transmission between a source system and destination system.
- **Tracert** = Displays the active path a node is using to contact another node. Will often display the following information about the nodes included in transit such as:
  1. IP address
  2. Fully Qualified Hostname
  3. Time of transmission
- **Arp –a** = Displays IP addresses associated with MAC addresses of any hosts to which there was a communication.
- **Nbtstat –a** = Displays a computers hostname via its ip address.
- **Route print** = Display paths a node can use to pass traffic to various sections on a network. Primary syntax used on Microsoft Command Line applications.
- **Sh IP Route** = Used to display paths a node can use to pass traffic to various sections on a network. Primary syntax used on Cisco Command Line applications.
- **Running-Configurations** = This is the "area" of RAM that network devices keep instructions and settings. This area is depending on electricity, however. If the network device loses power, all the settings disappear.

- **Startup-Configurations** = This "file" holds all the settings and customizations of a network device. This is in "flash" which allows the file to keep all settings and customizations without external electricity.

- **Network Management Software** = In order to configure and monitor the functions on network devices there is required a software interface. The software selected can provide access to multiple capabilities of a network device. Which management software selected can be either proprietary or the preference of a network technician. Below are some of the options available concerning management software:

  1. **Web Browser** = There are many varieties of web browsers such as "Chrome", Firefox", "Internet Explorer", "Safari", etc. Many manufacturers install "Web Server" control features into their network devices which allow access to the device simply by typing the device's IP address into the browser. Oftentimes, when using a browser, the browser interface is called a "WebUI" (Web User Interface). Various "Buttons" and "Icons" are used to activate or engage device services and functions. The advantage to using a browser is that no additional software is required to access a network device. In addition, as long as the device is on a network and has electricity, a connection can be initiated from any device which has a browser (i.e., laptop, cellphone, IP-based television, etc.). Unfortunately, utilizing a browser requires that a device has been configured with basic configurations (i.e., IP address, passwords, etc.). In addition, depending on the manufacturer, all of the devices features might not be available.

  2. **HyperTerminal** = This is one of the oldest software's used for configuring network devices. It was based upon using telephone modems. Using HyperTerminal, a laptop or desktop and a console cable, a technician is able to turn on a "Command Line Interface" (Also called "CLI" and looks like what is classically called "DOS") = Access to HyperTerminal between 1995 and 2006 was extremely easy. The software is a free download and came included with many operating systems. The software required no installation so it could be run off of any device from a folder. prompt). Using the CLI it is possible to configure all features because the majority of network technology devices are customized for CLI commands. In the later

years, other updated configuration software was released to compensate for the lack of security features in HyperTerminal.

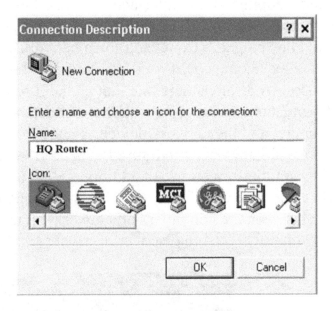

3. **TeraTerm** = This package has all the functions of HyperTerminal but many other enhancements over HyperTerminal. The user interface offers options concerning size of font, colors, tabbed views and many other superficial elements. In addition, there are many features critical in network device management such as Secure Shell (Called "SSH") which creates levels of encryption and security and Trivial File Transfer Protocol options (Called "TFTP") which allows the backup of configurations or the easy upload of the device operating systems. This allows use of configuration thru telnet, hypertext Transmission Protocol and the Console connection.

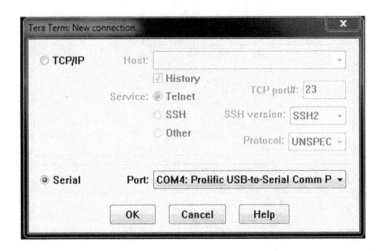

4. **Telnet** – Very popular during the initial growth and installation of network technology. This allows configuration of a network device using a command line interface embedded in many computer operating systems. Using unique commands, as long as the device could be "pinged" (Contacted) on a network via its IP address, using a CLI, a technician could perform almost all functions on network devices. A disadvantage to telnet is that it requires a "Server" and "Client" component to be installed and activated on both the access computer and the network device. In addition, the device would have to have already been configured with an IP address, passwords and other login information. In addition, telnet transmits information in what is termed as "Cleartext" which means that all typed commands sent between the computer and network device can be easily captured and "literally" read to discover passwords and other important data.

5. **Putty** = A free, open-source software used to configure varies network devices. In addition to provide multiple configuration, file transfer and encryption abilities. It provides other functions concerning encryption, compression and remote desktop.

Configure an IP Address (On Windows Systems)

While performing some exercises in this book, it will be required to configure Window Computer's with static IP addresses. There are two methods for establishing IP addresses on a Windows Computer. The two methods are as follows:

- **Graphical User Interface (GUI)**
- **Command Line Interface (CLI)**

Prior to any of the exercises,…we will have a brief discussion for both methods. Depending on the device or operating system, in order to communicate with other network devices there is the requirement for settings which allow transmission and reception of signals. In order for this to occur, devices have to share methods of communications commonly referred to as protocols. There are multiple protocols used in present network technology. The discussions in this text will primarily revolve around the protocol classified as TCP/IP (Transmission Control Protocol/Internet Protocol). This method of communication has two presently utilized version of version 4 and version 6. Much of our discussion will relate to version 4. In addition, many of the sections discussed will be directly related to Microsoft Operating Systems as well as the Cisco IOS.

When utilizing Windows operating systems in network environments, there are both GUI and CLI methods of viewing and manipulating network configurations. When using CLI, the command prompt is activated and then we will use the command IPCONFIG. When using this command in its smallest format, the CLI displays basic network settings.

```
C:\WINDOWS\system32\cmd.exe                              _ □ x

C:\>ipconfig

Windows IP Configuration

Ethernet adapter Local Area Connection 3:

        Media State . . . . . . . . . . . : Media disconnected
Ethernet adapter Local Area Connection 5:

        Media State . . . . . . . . . . . : Media disconnected
Ethernet adapter Wireless Network Connection 6:

        Connection-specific DNS Suffix  . :
        IP Address. . . . . . . . . . . . : 192.168.1.152
        Subnet Mask . . . . . . . . . . . : 255.255.255.0
        Default Gateway . . . . . . . . . : 192.168.1.1

C:\>
```

When performing the basic command of IPCONFIG the following are explanations of the display:

- **IP Address** = Decimal identity of computer on a TCP/IP network.
- **Subnet Mask** = Provides segmentation of groups of computers.
- **Default-Gateway** = Point which allows a section of a network to communicate with devices outside of that network.

The command also has optional modifications available which will show more specific displays of network configurations or allow the use of advanced features and tasks. In order to use the enhanced features, additional words and characters must be appended to the command. The character which must be added is often called a "Forward Slash" or a "Switch" normally represented by using "/". The "Switch" is followed by a number of other commands which can perform a number of operations. The most common enhanced command is by adding the "All" perimeter. This command will display a complete readout of all the settings presently used by the windows client as follows:

```
C:\WINDOWS\system32\cmd.exe                                          _ □

C:\>ipconfig /all

Windows IP Configuration

        Host Name . . . . . . . . . . . . : 3Com
        Primary Dns Suffix  . . . . . . . :
        Node Type . . . . . . . . . . . . : Hybrid
        IP Routing Enabled. . . . . . . . : No
        WINS Proxy Enabled. . . . . . . . : No
        DNS Suffix Search List. . . . . . : router.home

Ethernet adapter Local Area Connection 3:

        Media State . . . . . . . . . . . : Media disconnected
        Description . . . . . . . . . . . : Realtek PCIe GBE Family Controller
        Physical Address. . . . . . . . . : 40-09-4F-06-09-DD

Ethernet adapter Local Area Connection 5:

        Media State . . . . . . . . . . . : Media disconnected
        Description . . . . . . . . . . . : 3Com EtherLink XL 10/100 PCI For Com
plete PC Management NIC (3C905C-TX) #4
        Physical Address. . . . . . . . . : 00-09-4F-5F-DD-09-4F

Ethernet adapter Wireless Network Connection 6:

        Connection-specific DNS Suffix  . : router.home
        Description . . . . . . . . . . . : Belkin USB Adaptor
        Physical Address. . . . . . . . . : EC-09-4F-B0-B6-DD
        Dhcp Enabled. . . . . . . . . . . : Yes
        Autoconfiguration Enabled . . . . : Yes
        IP Address. . . . . . . . . . . . : 192.168.1.152
        Subnet Mask . . . . . . . . . . . : 255.255.255.0
        Default Gateway . . . . . . . . . : 192.168.1.1
        DHCP Server . . . . . . . . . . . : 192.168.1.1
        DNS Servers . . . . . . . . . . . : 192.168.1.1
        Lease Obtained. . . . . . . . . . : Saturday, August 12, 2007 7:40:59 AM

        Lease Expires . . . . . . . . . . : Sunday, August 13, 2007 7:40:59 AM

C:\>_
```

IP address are essential in network communications on TCP/IP networks. There are a number of methods utilized to establish address settings on network devices. The following are some of the options:

- **Static Address (Manual)** = This allows an IP address to be established by a technician. The technician can either use a CLI or GUI to manually type in an IP address. To set an IP address using CLI, the following could be done:
  1. **netsh interface ipv4 set address name="3Com19111" static 100.100.100.10 255.255.255.0 100.100.100.100**

The above command inserted "100.100.100.10" as the computer's IP address with a subnet mask of 255.255.255.0 and a default-gateway setting of 100.100.100.100. To set an IP address using the GUI, the following would be performed:

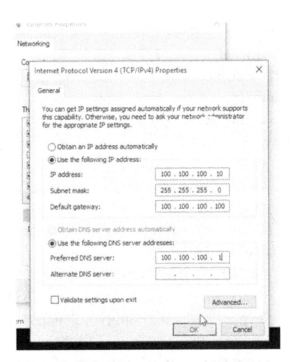

<u>Basic Hub, Switch and Router Configuration Practice:</u>

The following are some practical labs illustrating some methods of configuring network devices. All listed labs and exercises were created by using actual functioning PC's, Routers and Switches. Purchasing actual Routers and Switches is possible at a fraction of the cost by using "EBay" and "Amazon". Simulation software is also another option for practicing network technology tasks and activities. At the time of this book, there were a number of vendors who supplied simulation software such as "Boson NetSim", "NetSimK" and

"Packet Tracer". If simulation software is used,... some commands used on real devices may not work. Be sure to evaluate simulation software's available functions prior to attempting each lab.

Each lab builds on the prior labs so it is essential that they are completed in the order in which they appear. In addition, each lab increases in challenge levels and repeats prior activities in order to teach procedures and commands thru repetition. As the writer of this text, I would highly recommend completing each lab three times prior to starting the subsequent lab. When performing the lab for the third time, attempt to do so without any notes or instructions.

- **PC-Hub-PC** = This is the one of the first types of networks created for home offices. We will use two workstations and a hub. Afterwards we will confirm communications between the PC's. You will need the following for the lab:
  1) Two PC's with hardware ethernet connections (Not wireless!)
  2) PC's with Windows 7/8 or 10.
  3) 4 10/100/100 port hub (Inexpensive unit from 3Com or NetGear).
  4) Two straight ethernet cables.
  1. **Hardware Setup:**
     - ☐ Connect one straight cable from a PC to the hub.
     - ☐ Connect the remaining straight cable from the hub to the other PC.
  2. **Boot up each computer and access the command line interface (CLI).**
     - ☐ Got to the "Start" menu".
     - ☐ Click one time into the "Search" field.
     - ☐ Type "cmd" or "command" and the CLI "black-box" will appear.
  3. **Determine the network settings of each PC by doing the following:**
     - ☐ Type "ipconfig" in the command line option:
     - ☐ At least three lines of text will appear displaying the following:
       - • IPv4 address = This may appear as either of the following:
         - ➤ "0.0.0.0 = Means that the computer has not derived an IP address as of yet.

> 169.254.x.y = This is APIPA. The "x" and the "y" can be any number between 0 and 255. The will be different on each PC.

- IPv6 "link-local" address = Fe80: (Many numbers. This is for later so don't give this much attention).
- Subnet Mask = This attempts to identify the groups of computers which are associated for communications.
  > It should be 255.255.255.0
- Default Gateway = This should be blank at present.
- This first command attempts to show only "active" settings. To see all settings and connections regardless of status, the "ipconfig" command must be modified with a switch such as "/all". It is performed in the following manner, "ipconfig[space]/all". This command results in additional hardware and software settings. Settings important for our lab would include the following:
  > DNS Server = The device on the network which matches ip addresses to the hostname of systems.
  > DHCP Server = The device which distributes IP addresses to devices on a network (Will be empty for this lab).
  > Hostname = Written name of computer.
  > Physical Address = The hexadecimal mac address for the network adaptors on the system.

4. **Establish connections between PC's** = Using a command line tool, we can ascertain if the PC's can communicate with each other. Prior to attempting this command, assure all firewalls are off. If you are using a Windows PC. You can use a single command which will turn all firewalls off. To do so, activate the CLI and perform the command "netsh advfirewall set allprofiles state off". The command will respond with "OK" when the firewalls has been disabled. To re-enable the firewalls, simple type the same command but replace "off" with "on". (Note, this command will only work if Windows is

controlling the firewall and not a third-party software such as
Symantec or McAfee). After the firewall is down, we can
attempt communication tests. Perform the following steps:

- ☐ Identify each computer as computer "A" and computer
  "B".
- ☐ Using "ipconfig" record the ip address of each computer.
  Use the following as an example (Note if IP address
  reads "0.0.0.0" go to "Static Address Configuration):
  - Computer "A" = 169.254.182.10
  - Computer "B" = 169.254.112.20
- ☐ Access the CLI of computer "A".
- ☐ Type "ping" and the IP address of computer "B" such as
  "ping 169.254.112.20".
- ☐ The results should be between 3 and 5 sentences reading
  as follows:
  - Reply from 169.254.112.20: bytes = 32
    time=TTL= 32.
    - ➢ Just know that this means "Hey, I found the
      other computer!"
  - If you get any sentences stating, "Reply timeout"
    that means the target system cannot be located.

5. **Static IP Address Configuration** = Using APIPA is somewhat
   problematic for many of our labs, so we should use a static
   address. Depending on the operating system on the computer,
   there are different ways to access the network interface. We
   will use a simple command line to configure our network
   adaptor.
   - ☐ **Identify network interface** = Type in "ipconfig" and the
     active interface will appear with name of the interface
     and the ip address it is presently using.

```
C:\Users\rspencer>ipconfig

Windows IP Configuration

Wireless LAN adapter Wireless Network Connection 3:

   Media State . . . . . . . . . . . : Media disconnected
   Connection-specific DNS Suffix  . :

Wireless LAN adapter Wireless Network Connection 2:

   Connection-specific DNS Suffix  . :
   Link-local IPv6 Address . . . . . : fe80::b9d6:9590:92fb:3c8%15
   IPv4 Address. . . . . . . . . . . : 192.168.1.173
   Subnet Mask . . . . . . . . . . . : 255.255.255.0
   Default Gateway . . . . . . . . . : 192.168.1.10
```

❑ Using the interface name, we can configure an IP address on the interface using the following context:

```
Administrator: C:\Windows\system32\cmd.exe
C:\>netsh interface ipv4 set address name="local area connection 2" static 172.1
6.20.10 255.255.255.0 172.16.20.1
```

- **netsh interface ipv4 set address name="NameOfYourAdaptor" static ip-address subnet-mask gateway".** For our lab, go to computer "A" and perform the following:
  - ➢ netsh interface ipv4 set address name="NameOfYourAdaptor" static 172.16.20.10 255.255.255.0 172.16.20.1
  - ➢ Type "Ipconfig", again and check to see if the settings are what you expected.

❑ Go to computer "B" and perform the following:
  - ➢ netsh interface ipv4 set address name="NameOfYourAdaptor" static 172.16.20.20 255.255.255.0 172.16.20.1 (We have changed the last octet of the IP address to make "B" unique from "A".
  - ➢ Type "Ipconfig", again and check to see if the settings are what you expected.

❑ Execute pings between computer "A" and "B" looking for positive replies.
  - ➢ If you get positive replies, success!! You have created your first local area network! If not successful, check your firewalls and the IP addresses you placed on the individual computers.

❑ To return an interface to dhcp, perform the following:
  - ➢ netsh interface ipv4 set address name="NameOfYourAdaptor" source=dhcp

- **Terminal Emulator to Switch** = This lab will require the knowledge from all aspects of the previous lab. If you did not complete it, go back because instructions in this lab require the knowledge from the previous labs. Items required for this lab will be as follows:
  - Console cable

- Straight cable
- PC
- Corporate level switch (2600 or above with CLI).
- Terminal Emulation Software (TeraTerm/HyperTerminal/Putty) installed:

1. **Before starting, give the PC the following network settings:**
   - ☐ IP Address = 172.16.20.10
   - ☐ Subnet Mask = 255.255.255.0
   - ☐ Default Gateway = 172.16.20.1

2. **Switch Connection Process:**

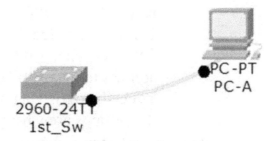

3. **Connect the end of the console cable to the PC using the "Serial" interface:**

4. **Connect the "RJ45" end into the Switch Console Port (Highlighted in "light" blue).**

5. Turn on terminal emulator and select correct port.

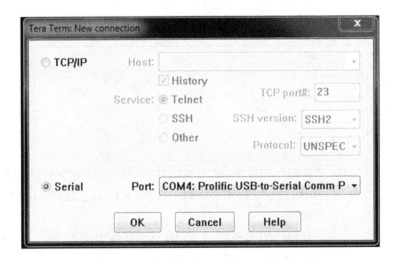

6. Hit the "Enter" key and you should be in " --- System Configuration Dialog ---"

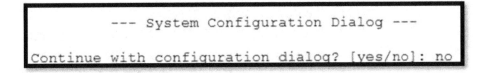

```
        --- System Configuration Dialog ---

Continue with configuration dialog? [yes/no]: no
```

7. Type "N" or "No" to all questions (About two or three). After you type the last "No" the system will check interfaces and circuitry and seem to stop. It is only waiting for your input.
8. Hit the "Enter" key and you should be in "User" mode (Indicated by the ">" prompt).
9. Type "Enable" or "en" and hit "enter" key to place you into "Privileged" mode (Indicated by the "#" prompt).
10. Evaluate the device by typing the following commands:
    - ☐ Sh ver = Displays the following:

- ➤ RAM usage
- ➤ Operating System Version
- ➤ Interfaces
- ➤ Platform
- ➤ Processor
- ➤ And present configuration register setting (We will talk about this item later in the book).

```
Cisco WS-C2950-24 (RC32300) processor (revision C0) with 21039K bytes of memory.

Processor board ID FHK0610Z0WC
Last reset from system-reset
Running Standard Image
24 FastEthernet/IEEE 802.3 interface(s)

63488K bytes of flash-simulated non-volatile configuration memory.
Base ethernet MAC Address: 0030.F218.E82A
Motherboard assembly number: 73-5781-09
Power supply part number: 34-0965-01
Motherboard serial number: FOC061004SZ
Power supply serial number: DAB0609127D
Model revision number: C0
Motherboard revision number: A0
Model number: WS-C2950-24
System serial number: FHK0610Z0WC
Configuration register is 0xF
```

- ☐ **Show run** = Will display, descriptions, customizations, interfaces and all configurations presently running on them.
- ☐ **Sh ip int brief** = Will display a small listing of network interfaces and their status.

11. **Began process for customizing the Switch with the following options:**
   - ☐ **Avoiding unknown command errors:**
      1) Switch>Enable
      2) Switch (Config t) (Moves into go Global Configuration).
      3) Switch (Config) # **no ip domain-lookup**
      4) Switch (Config) # end <enter> (This will move curser back to "User" mode.)
   - ☐ **Naming the Switch:**
      1) Switch>Enable
      2) Switch (Config t) (Moves into go Global Configuration).
      3) Switch (Config) # Hostname First_Floor_Switch (Immediately changes name of switch).

4) Switch (Config) # end <enter> (This will move curser back to "User" mode.)

☐ **Setting an IP address on Switch:**
   1) Switch> En
   2) Switch#
   3) Switch# Config t
   4) Switch (Config) # int vlan 1
   5) Switch (Config-if#) ip add 172.16.10.1 255.255.255.0
   6) Switch (Config-if#) no shut (This is an optional command)
   7) Switch (Config-if#) end <enter>
   8) Perform a "show run" or "Sh ip int brief" to see the IP listed.

☐ **Test connection between Switch and PC. From the CLI on the switch execute a "ping" to the PC:**
   1) First_Floor_S1> ping 172.16.20.2
   2) You should get a total of 5 exclamation points which = 100% successful. Other indications you could receive:
      ➢ "!" = 20% Successful
      ➢ "." = 20% Unsuccessful
      ➢ "U.U.U.U." = Destination unreachable or misconfiguration.
   3) Often the first time, only 60% is successful because device is learning network. Ping again and 100% should be the second result.

☐ **Removing an IP address:**
   1) Switch#Config-t (Moves into go Global Configuration).
   2) Switch (Config)# int vlan 1
   3) Switch (Config-if#) no ip add
   4) Switch (Config-if#) no shut (This is an optional command)
   5) Switch (Config-if#) end <enter>

☐ **To make a switch get IP address using DHCP:**
   1) Switch # Config-t (Moves into go Global Configuration).
   2) Switch (Config) # int vlan 1
   3) Switch (Config-if#) Ip add dhcp

4) Switch (Config-if#) no shut (This is an optional command)
5) Switch (Config-if#) end <enter>

- ☐ **Clearing all switch settings:**
  - ➢ There is no power button on a switch so to re-start it you must either:
  - ➢ Unplug and re-plug electrical cord or type the following in user mode:
  - ➢ Switch# Reload
  - ➢ A message may appear asking to save changes. Type "Y" for yes or "N" for no.

- **Switch-to-Switch** = This lab allows communication between two switches. To complete the tasks, you must be familiar with all previous labs. Remember to use commands to check your work (i.e., "Sh Run" and "Show IP int brief", etc.).
  1. Connect a Cross-over cable between the switches (Best practice although newer switches will auto-configure if a straight-cable is used).

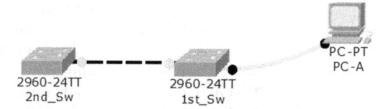

2960-24TT   2960-24TT
2nd_Sw   1st_Sw

  2. **Configure first switch as follows:**
     - ☐ Hostname = 1ST_Sw
     - ☐ IP Settings = 172.16.10.3 Netmask 255.255.255.0
  3. **Configure second switch as follows:**
     - ☐ Hostname = 2ND_Sw
     - ☐ IP Settings = 172.16.10.4 Netmask 255.255.255.0
  4. Ping between the two switch IP addresses.
  5. If pings fail, assure that devices are connected using Cisco Discovery Protocol.
     - ☐ On "1st_Sw enter "Privileged mode (#)".
     - ☐ Type "sh cdp neigh"
     - ☐ A display should appear stating that your neighbor is "2nd_Fl" and the port to which it is connected.

6. If you want to see a more detailed description, type in the expanded version of the CDP command, "Sh cdp neigh detail".
   - ☐ The result will display addition information such as IP address, operating system, platform, etc.

- **Switch and Router Passwords** = If a switch or router can be physically touched it is susceptible to access and reconfiguration. There are some methods which would make unauthorized access more difficult. We can configure some of these methods in the following ways:
  1. **Console Password** = This password protects the physical port used to connect the console cable (Also called "Rolled Cable" with the color of "Light Blue".). Before any terminal emulation software will allow access to a network device, a password must be entered and accepted. The following is the configuration process:
     - ☐ 1ST_Sw# sh run (Look for the statement which starts "…line con 0")
       ```
       line con 0
       !
       line vty 0 4
        login
       line vty 5 15
        login
       ```
     - ☐ 1ST_Sw# Config t
     - ☐ 1ST_Sw (Config)# line con 0
     - ☐ 1ST_Sw (Config)# Login (A message appears that a password is required but not set.)
     - ☐ 1ST_Sw (config-line)# Password getcon
     - ☐ 1ST_Sw (config-line)# End
     - ☐ 1ST_Sw#Sh run (Look for password related statements under "line con 0".)
     - ☐ Now turn off TeraTerm and re-plugging the console cable.
     - ☐ Restart Teraterm and hit enter (Notice a "User Access Verification" prompt appears).
       - ❖ Note: It will not show letters as you type.
     - ☐ Type in "getcon" and you are now in user mode of the switch.

2. **Enable Password** = This will stop users if they try to move from "user>" to "privileged#" mode. The following is the process:

- ☐ 1ST_Sw# sh run (Toward the "top half" of the screen, you will see no password statements).

```
Current configuration : 971 bytes
!
version 12.1
no service timestamps log datetime msec
no service timestamps debug datetime msec
no service password-encryption
!
hostname switch
```

- ☐ 1ST_Sw# Config t
- ☐ 1ST_Sw (Config)# enable password geten
- ☐ 1ST_Sw (config-line)# End
- ☐ 1ST_Sw# Sh run (Look for password towards top of readout)

```
Current configuration : 995 bytes
!
version 12.1
no service timestamps log datetime msec
no service timestamps debug datetime msec
no service password-encryption
!
hostname switch
!
enable password geten        <=
```

- ☐ 1ST_Sw# exit
- ☐ Hit enter
- ☐ 1ST_Sw> enable (Notice a "Password" prompt appears).
  - ❖ Note: It will not show letters as you type.
- ☐ Type in "geten" and press enter to access user mode of the switch.

3. **Telnet Password** = This allows remote access to a switch or router using an IP address. Prior to configuring telnet, an "Enable" password must be set. The process for telnet passwords are as follow:

- ☐ 1ST_Sw# sh run (Look for the statement which starts "…line vty 0 4 (Or 0 15)")

```
line con 0
!
line vty 0 4
 login
line vty 5 15
 login
```

- ☐ 1ST_Sw# Config t
- ☐ 1ST_Sw (Config)# line vty 0 4
- ☐ 1ST_Sw (Config)# Login (Messages may appears stating a password is required but not set on any lines)
- ☐ 1ST_Sw (config-line)# Password gettel
    - ❖ Note: Notice the prompted changed to "(config-line)#".
- ☐ 1ST_Sw (config-line)# End
- ☐ 1ST_Sw# Sh run (Look for password related statements under "line vty 0 4".)
- ☐ You must test the connection from another device such as a switch or a router. The other device must be able to successfully "ping" the switch or router you are attempting to access.
- ☐ 2ND_Sw # Ping 172.16.10.3 and wait for "!!!!! (100% Successful communications - Assuming this is the IP address of the switch we have enabled with telnet)."
- ☐ 2ND_Sw# telnet 172.16.10.3 (Notice a "User Access Verification" prompt appears).
- ☐ Type in "gettel" and press enter.
    - ❖ Note: It will not show letters as you type.
- ☐ Notice the prompt turns to the name of the switch we were attempting to access.
- ☐ 1ST_Sw>en
- ☐ You are now accessing the configurations of the other switch.

4. **Enable Secret** = All of the prior passwords are able to be read. The term for this is "cleartext". This is a security concern since configurations are often printed out to check settings. In order make systems more secure, we can restrict access to "privileged" mode by modifying the appearance of the enable

password to make it illegible. The term is called "encryption". In order to do this, you utilize the following method:

- ☐ 1ST_Sw# Config t
- ☐ 1ST_Sw (Config)# enable secret kitty
- ☐ 1ST_Sw (Config)# end
- ☐ 1ST_Sw# sh run (The password entry will now look like a random string of letters and numbers).

```
!
hostname switch
!
enable secret 5 $1$mERr$G6rRG3ftDWE7LtIkBa5Fx.
```

5. **Password Encryption** = In the previous lab, we encrypted the enable password. As in other labs, however, there are many other passwords on network devices which would still be legible such as the console or telnet passwords. There is a method to encrypt all passwords on a network device. The process is as follows:

- ☐ 1ST_Sw# Config t
- ☐ 1ST_Sw (Config)# service password-encryption
- ☐ 1ST_Sw (Config)# end
- ☐ 1ST_Sw# sh run (Now all passwords will appear as a random string of letters and numbers).

Chapter 9
Advanced Switch Configurations

Etherchannel:

The increased competition and demands on functionality caused by converged systems such as telephones, video systems, security of readers, etc., often overwhelms the bandwidth on sections of networks. This can result in broadcast storms or congestion due to bottlenecks originating on specific ports of network devices. Because of routing loop disabling technologies such as Spanning Tree Protocol it is not possible to simply connect multiple ports between network devices to allow a greater number of paths between connected devices. To circumvent Spanning Tree Protocol and allow multiple network connections between directly connected network devices there is an option utilize known as "Etherchannel". Etherchannel allows multiple connections between directly connected switches to be active simultaneously as well as combining the bandwidth of each connection into a greater total available bandwidth. To enable network devices to support Etherchannel it is a simple configuration as illustrated in the following paragraphs.

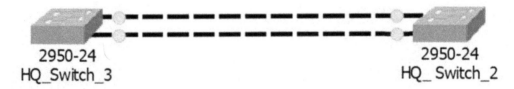

2950-24
HQ_Switch_3

2950-24
HQ_ Switch_2

- **Equipment to be used:**
  - At least two Cisco Switches with Etherchannel capability.
  - At least two crossover cables to connect Switches.

- **Etherchannel Setup:**
  1. Switch# show ip int brief (Displays at least one duplicated connection port is "shut (Disabled/Down".).
  2. Switch (config)# interface range FastEthernet0/10 – 11 (Identify all ports to support identical connections)
  3. Switch (config-if-range)# channel-group 5 mode active (Collects and activates ports into a combined collision domain)

Once configured Etherchannel information can be displayed by using either of the two commands below:
- show ip int brief (Displays all ports in channel are not "shut").
- show interfaces Port-channel 5 (Displays ports in Group 5)
- show etherchannel summary (shows every etherchannel)

Virtual Local Area Network Configuration (VLAN):

Configuring VLANs is a very good idea in order to reduce network congestion as well as created security areas. Vlan Names and numbers are case-sensitive so great care must be taken when attempting to create matching VLANs on different Switches.

- **2PC-to-Switch VLANs** = Virtual Local Area Networks are created and managed by switch software. Essentially, sections of memory are used to allow communications between specific computers. Multiple sections can be created which are not allowed to communicate to other sections. This creates a boundary of security between specific groups of computers.

- The following are commands required to configure a VLAN on a switch. Before starting, give two PC's the following network settings using "netsh" on the command line:

1. Computer "A":
    - ☐ IP Address = 172.16.20.10
    - ☐ Subnet Mask = 255.255.255.0
    - ☐ Default Gateway = 172.16.20.1
    - ☐ Interface = fa0/5
2. Computer "B":
    - ☐ IP Address = 172.16.20.20
    - ☐ Subnet Mask = 255.255.255.0
    - ☐ Default Gateway = 172.16.20.1
    - ☐ Interface = fa0/10
3. Go to computer "A" and open the CLI.
4. Ping computer "B" two times (The first ping may be 60% but the remainder will be 100%).
5. Now we will create a VLAN with the following commands:
    - ☐ 1ST_Sw# Config t
    - ☐ 1ST_Sw (Config)# vlan 20 (Gives the vlan a number reference)

□ 1ST_Sw (Config-vlan)# name staff (Optional to identify purpose).
□ 1ST_Sw (Config-vlan)# end

```
1ST_Sw#conf t
Enter configuration commands, one per line.  End with CNTL/Z.
1ST_Sw(config)#vlan 20
1ST_Sw(config-vlan)#name staff
1ST_Sw(config-vlan)#end
1ST_Sw#
%SYS-5-CONFIG_I: Configured from console by console
```

□ 1ST_Sw# sh vlan (Displays all vlans and associated interfaces).

```
1ST_Sw#sh vlan

VLAN Name                             Status     Ports
---- -------------------------------- ---------- -------------------------------
1    default                          active     Fa0/1, Fa0/2, Fa0/3, Fa
                                                 Fa0/5, Fa0/6, Fa0/7, Fa
                                                 Fa0/9, Fa0/10, Fa0/11,
                                                 Fa0/13, Fa0/14, Fa0/15,
                                                 Fa0/17, Fa0/18, Fa0/19,
                                                 Fa0/21, Fa0/22, Fa0/23,
                                                 Gig1/1, Gig1/2
20   staff                            active
1002 fddi-default                     act/unsup
1003 token-ring-default               act/unsup
1004 fddinet-default                  act/unsup
1005 trnet-default                    act/unsup
```

6. Now we will place one interface into VLAN 20:
   □ 1ST_Sw# Config t
   □ 1ST_Sw (Config)# int fa0/5
   □ 1ST_Sw (Config-if)# switchport access vlan 20
   □ 1ST_Sw (Config-if)# end
   □ 1ST_Sw# sh vlan (Shows interfaces in VLAN 20).

```
1ST_Sw#sh vlan

VLAN Name                             Status    Ports
---- -------------------------------- --------- ---------------
1    default                          active    Fa0/1, Fa0/2,
                                                Fa0/6, Fa0/7,
                                                Fa0/11, Fa0/12
                                                Fa0/15, Fa0/16
                                                Fa0/19, Fa0/20
                                                Fa0/23, Fa0/24
20   staff                            active    Fa0/5, Fa0/10
```

7. Go to computer "A" and open the CLI.
8. Ping computer "B" two times (The communication fails because they are not in a vlan).
9. Now we will place the other interface into VLAN 20:
   - ☐ 1ST_Sw (Config)# int fa0/10
   - ☐ 1ST_Sw (Config-if)# switchport access vlan 20
   - ☐ 1ST_Sw (Config-if)# end
   - ☐ 1ST_Sw# sh vlan (Shows interfaces in VLAN 20).
10. Go to computer "A" and open the CLI.
11. Ping computer "B" two times (The first ping may be 60% but the remainder will be 100%).

VLAN Propagation:

When switches are connected to one another, it is possible to have them automatically provide VLAN information to other switches. This process is called "VLAN propagation". This is extremely convenient on networks with dozens of switches. VLAN information can be centrally managed in the aspect that all creations, changes and deletions can be performed on one switch which are transmitted to the other switches. Due to VLAN properties on switches,…changes are only allowed on particular switches while others can either participate or totally ignore VLAN configurations. The following are some of the attributes of VLAN propagation:

- **Virtual Trunking Protocol (VTP)** = Software which allows VLAN creation and data propagation.
- **VTP Domains** = This defines the switches who participate in VLAN propagation. A domain is indicated by a specific "Name" and all switches that exchange VLAN information will have this name in their database. A

domain can also have "password" settings to limit which switches are allowed to receive domain information.

- **VTP Server** = This defines the switch which allows the adding, changing and modification of VLAN information.
- **VTP Client** = This defines a switch which can only receive VLAN information. No changes of any type can be performed on this switch.
- **VTP Transparent** = This mode is often used on a switch that exists in a VTP domain but does not participate in VLAN propagation. In addition, other VLAN's can be created on this switch but they will not be communicated to other switches.
- **Default/Black Hole VLAN** = This is the default vlan all switches use on startup without configuration. After VLANS are created, this vlan is often degraded so no vlan traffic passes thru it (This is why it is also called the "Black Hole").

The following is a process for configuring and manipulating a VTP domain. It will be necessary to have performed all previous exercises before attempting this lab. You will need the following:

- Single Cross-Over Cable.
- Four PC's with the following network settings:
- Connect Computer "A" to 1ST_ SW using a straight cable with the following settings:
  1. IP Address = 172.16.20.10
  2. Subnet Mask = 255.255.255.0
  3. Default Gateway = 172.16.20.1
  4. Interface = fa0/3
- Connect Computer "B" to 1ST_SW using a straight cable with the following settings:
  1. IP Address = 172.16.20.20
  2. Subnet Mask = 255.255.255.0
  3. Default Gateway = 172.16.20.1
  4. Interface = fa0/4
- Connect Computer "C" to 2ND_ SW using a straight cable with the following settings:
  1. IP Address = 172.16.30.10
  2. Subnet Mask = 255.255.255.0
  3. Default Gateway = 172.16.30.1
  4. Interface = fa0/3

- Connect Computer "C" to 2ND_ SW using a straight cable with the following settings:
    1. IP Address = 172.16.30.20
    2. Subnet Mask = 255.255.255.0
    3. Default Gateway = 172.16.30.1
    4. Interface = fa0/4
- Two Switches (With at least 12 ports) with hostnames of:
    1. 1ST_SW with VLAN 1 IP address 172.16.10.2
    2. 2ND_SW with VLAN 1 IP address 172.16.10.3

```
1ST_Sw#conf t
Enter configuration commands, one per line.  End with CNTL/Z.
1ST_Sw(config)#int vlan 1
1ST_Sw(config-if)#ip add 172.16.10.2 255.255.255.0
1ST_Sw(config-if)#no shut

1ST_Sw(config-if)#
%LINK-5-CHANGED: Interface Vlan1, changed state to up
```

- **VTP Domain and VLAN configuration Process** = Perform the following steps on 1ST_Sw:
    1. **Sh run** = This shows any interfaces which are part of vlans.
    2. **Sh vlans** = This command displays the existence of all VLANs and which interfaces are participated in them.
    3. **Sh vtp status** = Displays the name of VTP domains, switch status (Server/Client), changes to VLAN's and indicator of the VTP Server for domain.
    4. **Conf t** = Moves from Privileged to Global Configuration Mode.
    5. **vtp mode server** = Will make the switch the server for the VTP domain.
        - ☐ Note: All switches are in "Server" mode by default so you will get a message indicated the fact. This step is simply "Best Practice".
    6. **Vtp domain mydomain1** = Will create the domain with the name "mydomain1".
    7. **Exit** = Terminates Global Configuration Mode.

```
1ST_Sw#conf t
Enter configuration commands, one per line.  End with CNTL/Z.
1ST_Sw(config)#vtp mode server
Device mode already VTP SERVER.
1ST_Sw(config)#vtp domain mydomain1
Changing VTP domain name from NULL to mydomain1
1ST_Sw(config)#exit
1ST_Sw#
%SYS-5-CONFIG_I: Configured from console by console
```

8. Sh vtp status = You will now see the name "mydomain1" in the domain of the status and the IP address of the switch in the "configuration last modified" section.

```
1ST_Sw#sh vtp status
VTP Version                       : 2
Configuration Revision            : 0
Maximum VLANs supported locally   : 255
Number of existing VLANs          : 6
VTP Operating Mode                : Server
VTP Domain Name                   : mydomain1
VTP Pruning Mode                  : Disabled
VTP V2 Mode                       : Disabled
VTP Traps Generation              : Disabled
MD5 digest                        : 0xED 0x52 0x62 0x45 0xE5 0x47 0x
```

- Create vlan on 1st_Sw:
    1. 1ST_Sw (Config)# Vlan 20
    2. 1ST_Sw (Config-vlan)# Name red
    3. 1ST_Sw (Config-vlan)# Exit
    4. 1ST_Sw (Config)# Vlan 30
    5. 1ST_Sw (Config-vlan)# Name green
    6. 1ST_Sw (Config-vlan)# End
    7. 1ST_Sw# Sh vtp status (You notice that the number of vlans has increased and the Configuration Revision number increased by each VLAN command we entered).
- Configure 2nd_Sw:
    1. 2nd_Sw# Sh vlans (Notice only the default 5 vlans exist.).
    2. Configure the trunked port:
        ➢ 2nd_Sw# Conf t
        ➢ 2nd_Sw (Config)# Int fa0/1

> ➤ 2nd_Sw (Config-if)# Switchport mode trunk (Instructs port to allow all vlans to communicated thru that specific port)
3. End

```
1ST_Sw#conf t
Enter configuration commands, one per line.  End with CNTL/Z.
1ST_Sw(config)#int fa0/1
1ST_Sw(config-if)#switchport mode trunk
```

4. 2nd_Sw# Sh run = Interface fa0/1 should have a "Switchport mode trunk" statement beneath it.

```
1ST_Sw#sh run
Building configuration...

Current configuration : 1127 bytes
!
version 12.2
no service timestamps log datetime msec
no service timestamps debug datetime msec
no service password-encryption
!
hostname 1ST_Sw
!
!
!
!
spanning-tree mode pvst
!
interface FastEthernet0/1
 switchport mode trunk
!
interface FastEthernet0/2
!
```

5. Sh vtp status (The defaults of Server and 5 vlans should exist.)
6. Vtp mode client (Sets the mode of Switch in VTP domain)
7. Vtp domain my domain1 (Creates the name of the domain).
8. Sh vtp status (New settings now exist with no settings for Last Configuration from and the "Configuration Revision" number is 0.)
- Connect 1ST_SW Fa0/1 to 2ND_SW Fa0/2 using a crossover cable and wait 3 minutes.
  1. 2nd_Sw# Sh vlans (Both red and green vlans have been duplicated.)
  2. 2nd_Sw# Sh vtp status (The "Last Configuration" IP address reflects that 1st_Sw is the VTP Server and the revision number is identical to the number which exists on the VTP Server.)

3. New VLANs can only be added on the VTP Server. If you try to add vlans on the VTP client, it does not accept the commands and instructs that creation is not allowed on the client.
4. At this stage, ports can be placed into vlans. This was done in a previous lab so refer to the previous lab for instructions on placing ports into vlans.

Spanning Tree Protocol (STP):

Most network infrastructures have many switches connected to one another in series. Often times, multiple connections can accidently be created between switches. This scenario can result in what is called a "Routing Loop" which allows frames and packets to continually repeat their path without attempting another path or finding their destination. If frames and packets do not find their network, they will not allow room for new packets to enter the network resulting in the degradation and slowing down of network processes and bottlenecks. In order to reduce the chances of frames looping the network, there is a protocol entitled "Spanning Tree Protocol (STP)". This protocol allows the switches to exchange data about paths and disables any connections which would allow a redundant path to exist between switches. STP is supported by "Bridge Protocol Data Unit (BPDU)" Guard which can be enabled on switches to assist the establishment of best paths towards the Root Bridge. This is an additional option when using Spanning Tree Protocol. The commands to activate BPDU Guard are as follows:
1. Int fa0/#
2. spanning-tree bpduguard enable

Root Bridge:

Switches enabled with STP will attempt to automatically disable routing loops by selecting the switch with the lowest mac address as the "Root Bridge (The switch in charge of identifying all the paths between switches). Best practice is for the network administrator to manually assign whichever switch is closest to the Main Router in the network as the Root Bridge. The following are the commands used to establish the Root Bridge:

- **STP and Root bridge with Three Switches:**
  1. Lab Setup: Three switches connected with crossover cables and the following IP addresses:
     - Sw_1 = 172.16.10.2
     - Sw_2 = 172.16.10.3

➤ Sw_3 = 172.16.10.4

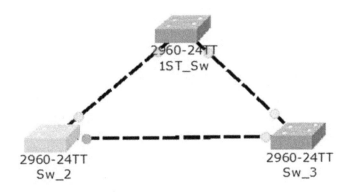

2. View present STP settings on each switch:
   ➤ **Sh spanning-tree** = Displays vlans on the switch, which switch is the "Root Bridge" and the present state of ports connected to other switches.
   ➤ On one of the switches, after running "Sh spanning-tree", you will see "This bridge is the root" after the VLAN statement:

```
Sw_1#sh spanning-tree
VLAN0001
  Spanning tree enabled protocol ieee
  Root ID    Priority    32769
             Address     000A.F365.49B7
             This bridge is the root
             Hello Time  2 sec  Max Age 20 sec  Forward Delay 15 sec
```

3. **Let's move the Root bridge to another switch:**
   ➤ Select any switch that did not state it was the root bridge. You can identify that it is not a bridge because it does not indicate statements about being a bridge.
   ➤ Record the name of the VLANs it displays (Note: Root Bridges are based per VLAN, not per switch. A switch can have multiple VLAN's on it, the network administrator would have to identify for which VLAN the specific switch would be the Root Bridge).
   ➤ Perform the following steps on a switch that is NOT A ROOT BRIDGE:

```
Sw_2#sh spanning-tree
VLAN0001
  Spanning tree enabled protocol ieee
  Root ID    Priority    32769
             Address     000A.F365.49B7
             Cost        19
             Port        1(FastEthernet0/1)
             Hello Time  2 sec  Max Age 20 sec  Forward Delay 15 sec
```

> ➢ Execute the command which will make this a bridge:
> ❖ spanning-tree vlan 1 root primary

```
Sw_2(config)#spanning-tree vlan 1 root primary
```

- Show Spanning Tree (Displays that this switch is now the Root Bridge for VLAN 1.)
- Go back to the switch which possessed the root bridge previously and it now is gone. Practice with the commands by moving the Root Bridge status to another switch.

The primary reason of utilizing Root Bridges is to support streamlined communications from the network to the primary routing devices such as an organizations router. For better clarity, let's look at another situation in which the Root Bridge locations is more easily seen as a problem in network communications. Most network infrastructures have many switches connected to one another in series. Often times, multiple connections can accidently be created between switches. This scenario can result in what is called a "Routing Loop" which allows frames and packets to continually repeat their path without attempting another path or finding their destination. If frames and packets do not find their network, they will not allow room for new packets to enter the network resulting in the degradation and slowing down of network processes and bottlenecks. In order to reduce the chances of frames looping the network, there is a protocol entitled "Spanning Tree Protocol (STP)". This protocol allows switches to exchange data about paths and disables connections which would allow redundant paths to exist between switches. Switches enabled with STP will attempt to automatically disable routing loops by selecting the switch with the lowest MAC address as the "Root Bridge (The switch in charge of identifying all the paths between connected switches). The Root Bridge is often automatically determined by STP based on any combination of the switch with the greatest hours of uptime or the lowest MAC address. The protocol make an assumption that the switch with the lowest MAC address is the oldest and has been in operation the longest which provides potential of the most expansive MAC address table for path purposes. This can be a determent to a network however because of modification of network infrastructure or switch replacement. Best practice is for the network administrator to manually assign whichever Root Bridge status to a switch. If this is not done, there is great potential that congestion can result within the network as packets are attempting to find their way to the primary distribution point on the network which is often a router. Take the following scenario for example:

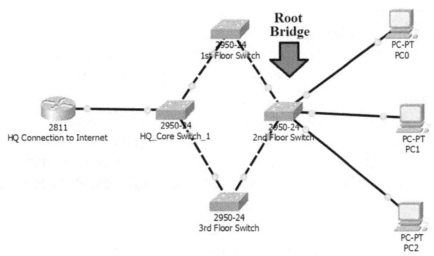

In this situation the Root Bridge exists on the 2nd Floor switch. In a small network of this size it would not cause much difficulty. If this network were to include 40 more switches however and the HQ Connection to the Internet actually existed in a different building such as a college campus there would be extreme delays and broadcast storms experienced daily. The best solution would be to make the HQ Core Switch the Root Bridge. The following are commands used to establish a Root Bridge:

- **Equipment to be used (Just Essentials):**
  o At least 4 Cisco Switches
  o Associated cross-over cables for connections.

- **STP and Root bridge with Three Switches** = In this example the switches are connected with crossover cables and the following IP addresses:
  ➤ HQ Core Switch 1 = 172.16.10.2
  ➤ 1st Floor Switch = 172.16.10.3
  ➤ 2nd Floor Switch = 172.16.10.4
  ➤ 3rd Floor Switch = 172.16.10.5

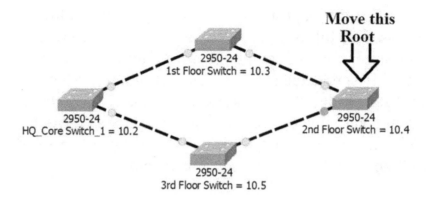

- **Switch Configurations:**
    1. Sh spanning-tree (Displays vlans on the switch, which switch is the "Root Bridge" and the present state of ports connected to other switches.)
        ➤ The readout on the 2nd Floor Switch will display "This bridge is the root" after the VLAN statement (Note: Root Bridges are based per VLAN, not per switch. A switch can have multiple VLAN's on it and each can have a different Root Bridge).

```
#sh spanning-tree
VLAN0001
  Spanning tree enabled protocol ieee
  Root ID    Priority    32769
             Address     000A.F365.49B7
             This bridge is the root
             Hello Time  2 sec  Max Age 20 sec
```

   ➤ The readout on any other Switch will not display the "Bridge" statement indicating that it is not the root.

```
#sh spanning-tree
VLAN0001
  Spanning tree enabled protocol ieee
  Root ID    Priority    32769
             Address     0001.4333.2500
             Cost        19
             Port        24(FastEthernet0/24)
             Hello Time  2 sec  Max Age 20 sec
```

   2. (config)#spanning-tree vlan 1 root primary (Makes HQ Core Switch the Root Bridge.)

After configuring HQ Core Switch 1, perform the "sh spanning-tree" command which displays that this switch is now the Root Bridge for VLAN 1. If you go back to 2nd Floor switch you will notice that the "root bridge" statement is gone.

In larger networks, it is best practice to create another root bridge in case the single one fails to function. To create a backup root bridge you would use the "spanning-tree vlan 1 root secondary" command.

In some cases, there is the need to disable STP. This is normally the situation in which it is assured that a port on a switch is connected to an end device such as a phone, computer or printer. In this case, there would be no need for the interface to collect multiple device MAC addresses which might be reached thru the port because the port will only have one device connected to it. This configuration would reduce processing and RAM utilization on the switch. To configure this port condition it is necessary to active "PortFast". Portfast customizes ports to communicate directly with end devices such as computers, IP phones, printers, etc.. Port Fast is only to be configured on ports connected to end devices and never another switch or router. Once a port has this setting it will not add additional MAC entrees for path purposes. If another switch is connected to a port configured with Portfast any section of that network will be unreachable. To enable the setting the following steps are required:
1. Int fa0/#
2. spanning-tree portfast

Chapter 10
Introduction to Routers

Introduction to Routers:

Routers connect to the "Backbone" of public and private networks. Traditionally, every building which has an internet connection has at least one router which is connected in "series" to an internet service provider (ISP). In turn, the ISP is connected to a POP (Point of Presence) which is subsequently connected to the DOD (Department of Defense). From the DOD there are thousands of routers which traverse the planet appearing on land, under the sea and in orbit comprising various portions of the Internet. In order to allow communications between the various devices, routers must either learn or be taught about network devices to which they are connected as well as the devices which are connected to their closest neighbors. The methods used by routers range in complexity and specific function. The following are some of the elements involved in configuring routers.

- **Interface port types** = Many routers have ports identical to those of a Switch such as Ethernet type (i.e., Fastethernet), fiber, aux, console, etc. In addition, routers also have other ports which are utilized to connect to other routers or an internet service provider such as:
  1. **Serial** = Serial interfaces are high-speed WAN connections which utilize various connector types such as Frame Relay, ISDN, T1, T3 and others. Typically, these connections will bridge the distance between buildings or from a particular building to an ISP (Internet Service Provider).
  2. **Attachment Unit Interface** = Legacy connection for routers.

Router Configurations Exercises:

Configuring a router is almost identical to working with a switch. There are a few different commands, but essential functions are the same as in the prompts, names and concepts. Each time new commands are introduced, they will be displayed in **BOLD** text. In order to complete the following labs, it would have been necessary to complete all prior labs. If you did not, go back to the labs for switches and complete them or there will be a lack of understanding concerning configuring routers. For this lab you will need the following:

- Console cable
- Terminal software of your choice (Teraterm/Putty/HyperTerminal)
- Router (1800 series or higher)
- Computer with Windows 7, 8 or 10.
- We begin the process by examining router settings. Activate the terminal emulation software and run the following commands:
  1. --- System Configuration Dialog ---type "No" and enter.

```
        --- System Configuration Dialog ---

Continue with configuration dialog? [yes/no]:
```

- From here, you will be able to use commands we have used on switches such as:
  1. Hostname
  2. Copy run start
  3. To get started, perform the following:
  4. Enable
  5. Sh ver = Displays license, operating system, RAM and boot settings.
  6. Show run = Displays all connections, interfaces, settings and present configurations established on the router. Any interface which is not activated will show the word "Shutdown" after the name of the interface.
  7. Sh ip int brief = Displays network communication interfaces on the router and their status.

```
Router1#sh ip int brief
Interface              IP-Address      OK? Method Status                Protocol

FastEthernet0/0        unassigned      YES unset  administratively down down

FastEthernet0/1        unassigned      YES unset  administratively down down

Serial0/0/0            unassigned      YES unset  administratively down down

Serial0/0/1            unassigned      YES unset  administratively down down
```

Router-to-PC:

In this lab, we will configure a router to communicate with a workstation. The workstation will be both a part of a small "network" and the primary system to configure the router.

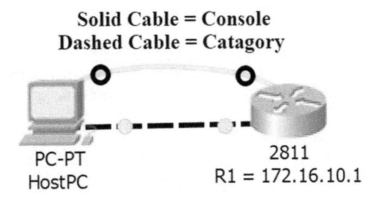

Solid Cable = Console
Dashed Cable = Catagory

PC-PT
HostPC

2811
R1 = 172.16.10.1

The following are some of the helping commands which will be used on this lab:

8. **Ctrl-c** = Move out of Global Configuration mode and return to privileged.
9. **Ctrl-z** = Apply the present command to running config and move to privileged.
10. **Ctrl+Shift+6 (X)** = Stops the router from attempting to process an incorrect command.
11. **No IP domain-lookup** = Stops the router from attempting to associate DNS information to an incorrect command input.
12. **End** = Move back to privileged mode.
13. **Exit** = Move one command back.
14. **Reload** = Will cause the router to reboot:
    ➢ If any changes were made, the router will prompt if the additional settings should be saved. Press "Yes" and continue to reboot router.

- Make sure all firewalls on the PC are off. You will have to configure the Workstation with the following settings:
  1. Host IP = 172.16.10.10 Subnet 255.255.255.0 (We are using classless)
  2. Default Gateway for PC = 172.16.10.1
  3. DNS Server = 172.16.10.100 (This performs no actual function for our labs and is simply a "place holder" for now).

- The following commands will be performed on "Router1":
    1. **Conf t** = Moves from Privileged to Global Configuration Mode.
    2. **IP classless** = This will allow the router to use both "Classfull" and "Classless" IP and Subnet combinations.
    3. We will use the "Ethernet" type interface on the router to connect to the PC.

- Configure the router as follows:
    1. **Sh ip int brief** = Displays interfaces. We will select the "FastEthernet0/0" (Which we will abbreviate with "Fa0/0").
    2. **Conf t**
    3. **Int fa0/0**
    4. **(Conf-if) ip add 172.16.10.1 255.255.255.0** = This command sets the IP address and turns on the protocol TCP/IP.
    5. **(Conf-if) no shut** = This command turns on the interface.
    6. End
    7. **Sh run** = Displays the interface but the "shutdown" statement is gone indicating the interface is activated.
    8. **Sh ip int brief** = Now the Fa0/0 displays an IP address but there is an entry which reads "protocol down" because the interface is not presently connected to anything.
    9. Connect a "crossover" cable from the routers "Fa0/0" to the computers network interface. Your terminal emulator software will now begin displaying messages reading "up" indicating that the interface is connected to a device.
        - Note: Normally, PC's are connected to Switches which are then connected to Routers. For our lab activities, we are "bending" network best practices. This action then requires a "cross-over "cable to allow communications. Many newer routers have software on the ports which recognizes the cable being used,… and will modify the ports automatically to allow communication, however. It is always best practice, however to simply use a cross-over in any situation which is normal.
    10. **Sh ip int brief** (Now the Fa0/0 displays an IP address and also has two "up" statements meaning that the interface is now fully activated.)
    11. **Ping from router to PC using "Ping 172.16.10.10"** = Should show at least three exclamation points (!). Do again to give a total of 5.

Descriptions on Interfaces:

Working with multiple interfaces on a router (or switch) it is difficult to keep track of their connections and to what they terminate. An option available on interfaces is to write an actual name on an interface called a "description". The following is an example of setting a description on an interface:

12. Conf t
13. Int fa0/0
14. (Conf-if) description Connection to PC
15. End
16. Sh run = This command displays what is known as the "Running Configurations". When you get to the Fa0/0 interface it will have the sentence "Connection to PC" beneath the interface indicator.

- **Saving Configurations** = By default, routers will not automatically save any changes made to them. In order to assure the router will remember the configurations which have been established,…you must make the router save the running settings into the startup file for the router. This file is normally referred to as the "Config.text" file. In order to update the "Config.text" you must tell the router to move the "Running Configurations" into the "Config.text" as "Startup Configurations". The command "Copy run start" will save the settings for the next restart:

- **Configuration Register** = Holds settings which controls the behavior of the router when it boots. The Configuration register can be accessed by interrupting the boot sequence prior to its completion. This is done either by using a "Ctrl+Break" key combination or issuing the "Break" option on Tera Term or Putty. Once a Boot Interruption is active, the prompt will appear as " >" on a Router or "Switch:>" on a switch. Once there, it is possible to use the "confreg (0x000)" command indicating how the system should boot. After entering the command, it is necessary to restart the device by using a "reset" command. There are a number of settings which are for normal operation or troubleshooting as in the following:
  1. **0x2100 or 0x0** = Boots ROM Monitor for troubleshooting.
  2. **0x2101 or 0x1** = Boots RXBoot Code\Boot helper image\Mini OS will load from ROM 0x2102 or 0x2 or 0xF = Boot from FLASH using NVRAM's start-configs
  3. **0x2142** = Boot from FLASH skipping NVRAM's start-configs.
     4. Great for password recovery.

Chapter 11
Network Topologies

Network Topologies:

This term identifies the anticipated design or the existing arrangement of devices on a network. Servers, cables, rooms, routers, switches and many other devices can be included in the layout of the network topology. Often times, different parts of the network may be evaluated in a manner which requires only specific elements of the network to be displayed. When this occurs, a subset of a topology is created called a "Network Decomposition" which filters out anything extraneous to the aspects of the network elements under evaluation. At the root levels, there are two essential levels of a network topology. Those would be the "Logical" topology and the "Physical" topology.

- **Logical** = This network decomposition lists the identities of network devices in groups. Presently, an accepted standard is to utilize the IP addresses of nodes and hosts in reference to their associations and establishing which part of the network in which the device resides. Additional descriptions and symbols identifying items such as firewalls, e-mail servers and domain controllers often accompany many of the characteristics of a Logical Topology. Below are some examples:

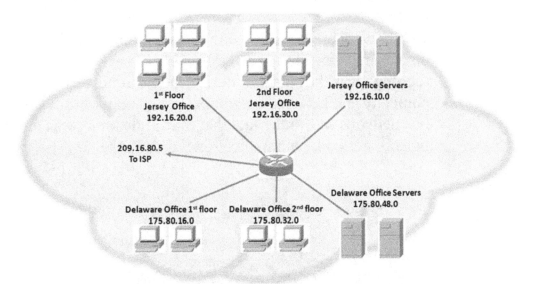

Company WAN example

- **Physical** = This network composition identities how devices are physically connected to one another based on cables, wireless and other connection media. There are characteristics of actual distance and proximity of devices. In addition, the arrangement of media connections are also highlighted on physical topologies which results in various names for specific designs. Below are some examples of Physical Topologies:

➤ **LAN (Local Area Network)** = Network which includes communication connected computers within close proximity of one another such as a room or building

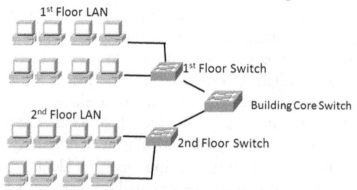

➤ **MAN (Metropolitan (or "Medium") Area Network)** = Collection of connected LANS spanning the territory of a complex, campus or city.

➤ **WAN (Wide Area Network)** = This network is a collection of connected MANS which are separated by large geographic distances such as in state to state or country to country. One of the best examples of a WAN is the internet.

➤ **BUS** = Network setup in which each computer and network device are connected to a single cable or backbone. This topology was the standard during the beginning of most company and building networks. The primary disadvantage to a bus network was in the fact that if a single break was on the line, all network communication would cease.

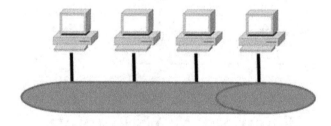

➤ **RING** = A circular design for a network in which a PDU travels from one node to the next in a specific sequence. In the early implementations of this topology, the PDU only traveled in a single direction. If there was a single break in the line, all communications would stop.

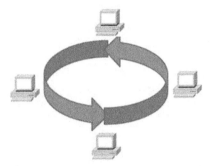

> **STAR** = Using a "Central Point" for communications, all nodes are connected via the central point which is often a hub or a switch. The PDU travels independently of the number of nodes and the failure of any node will not disrupt the others. The single disadvantage in this topology is that the central point is very critical if it fails, the entire network will not operate.

> **MESH** = This topology is the most stable. Essentially, every node as more than one connection to all the other nodes. Using this connection style the network can continue operating with multiple failures in connection lines or nodes. The primary disadvantage to this topology is the redundancy increases the cost of the network due to the duplicated lines and devices.

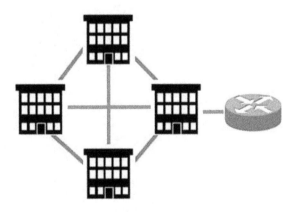

Chapter 12
Wide Area Network
Connection Methods

Wide Area Network Connection Methods:

In this lab, we will use interfaces traditionally used to connect routers or to connect routers to an Internet Service Provider (ISP). These interfaces are called "Serial". There are a few additional steps in configuring "Serial" interfaces which are not used for FastEthernet connections. One difference between Ethernet and serial connections is that the "Clock Rate" command must be used on one end of the cable to identify which interface is responsible for periodically checking the status of the connection. This lab also requires the mastery of all previous labs. In the event the previous labs have not been completed, go back and do so.

2811   2811
R1 = 172.16.20.1   R2 = 172.16.20.2

- On Router1 = Configure the router as follows:
  1. **Conf t**
  2. **(Config)# IP classless** (This will allow the router to use both "Classfull" and "Classless" IP and Subnet combinations.)
     ➢ We will use the "Serial" type interface on the routers.
  3. **Sh ip int brief** (Displays interfaces. We will select the "Serial 0/0" (Which we will abbreviate with "S0/0")).
  4. **Conf t**
  5. **(Config)# Int S0/0**
  6. **Clock rate 56000** (This is one of the base (Slowest) speeds used on serial interfaces to confirm connection status. This command also identifies the connection as a "DCE (Data Clocking Equipment)").
     ➢ This end initiates the connection status signals.
  7. **(Config-if) ip add 172.16.20.1 255.255.255.0** (This command sets the IP address and turns on the protocol TCP/IP.)
  8. **(Config-if) no shut** (This command turns on the interface.)
  9. **End**
  10. **Sh run** (Displays the interface but the "no shutdown" statement is gone indicating the interface is activated.)
  11. **Sh ip int brief** (Now the S0/0 displays an IP address but there is an entry which reads "protocol down" because the interface is not presently connected to anything.)

- On Router2:
  1. **Conf t**
  2. **IP classless** (This will allow the router to use both "Classfull" and "Classless" IP and Subnet combinations)
  3. **Sh ip int brief** (Displays interfaces. We will select the "Serial 0/1" (Which we will abbreviate with "S0/1")).
  4. **Conf t**
  5. **(Config)# Int S0/1**
  6. **(Config -if) ip add 172.16.20.2 255.255.255.0** (This command sets the IP address and turns on the protocol TCP/IP.)
  7. **(Config-if) no shut**
  8. **Sh run** (Displays the interface but the "no shutdown" statement is gone indicating the interface is activated.)
     - Note = Notice there is no clock rate on this interface. Since the other end of the cable connected to Router 1 has had commands implemented to make the interface a DTE,…the other end (Which is on Router 2) now becomes a "DTE (Data Terminating Equipment). This occurs if there is NO CLOCK RATE applied to the serial interface. On all serial connections, one end is a DTE while the other is a DCE (The end of the cable which will respond to connection status).
  9. **End**
  10. Connect a "serial" cable between the routers "S0/0" and "S0/1". Your terminal emulator software will now begin displaying messages reading "up" indicating that the interface is connected to a device.
  11. Sh ip int brief = Now the S0/0 and the S0/1 on the routers display an IP address and also has two "up" statements meaning that the interfaces are now fully activated.
  12. Confirming connected Cisco devices (i.e., Routers and/or Switches) can be accomplished by using the "Cisco Discovery Protocol (CDP)" which is enabled on interfaces. Essentially, as long as electricity is activated on an interface, it will begin collecting data concerning what is connected to it. The interface does not need to have an IP address associated with it. There are a number of options for CDP commands as in the following:
      - **Sh cdp** = Will display if the protocol is running and when it will check the interface next.

☐ **sh cdp neighbors** = Will list all directly connected devices and a limited display of interfaces, device types, device hostnames and model numbers.

☐ **sh cdp neighbors det** = Detailed display of connected systems including IP addresses, operating systems and much more.

- On either router:
    1. **Sh cdp** = See timers and versions.
    2. **Sh cdp neigh det** = In depth display.
    3. **Ping from Router1 to Router2 using "Ping 172.16.20.1"** (Should show at least three exclamation points (!). Do again to display a total of 5 successful communications of 100%).

WAN Configuration Exercise:

The following lab will require the following routers. The following labs require the mastery of previous exercises. The identifiers for the serial interfaces on your routers (Such as "S0/0/0" or "S0/1" might be different, but any serial interfaces can be used. Just keep track of the interfaces you actually use. The following configurations must exist on the routers prior to attempting the lab:

- Router on Left:
    1. **IP classless** (Optional)
    2. **No ip domain-lookup** (Optional)
    3. **Hostname LR**
    4. S0/0/0 (DCE-56000), IP Address = 172.16.20.1 255.255.255.0 Connected to MM S0/0/1
- Router in Middle:
    1. Hostname MR
    2. No ip domain-lookup (Optional)
    3. IP classless (Optional)
    4. S0/0/1 (DTE) IP Address = 172.16.20.2 255.255.255.0 Connected to LR S0/0
    5. S0/0/0 (DCE-56000), IP Address = 172.16.30.1 255.255.255.0 Connected to RR. S0/1
- Router on Right:
    1. Hostname RR
    2. No ip domain-lookup
    3. IP classless (Optional)
    4. S0/0/1 (DTE), IP Address = 172.16.30.2 255.255.255.0 Connected to MR S0/0

- On MR:
  1. **Sh cdp neigh** (Displays connections to LR and RR.)

```
RM#sh cdp neigh
Capability Codes: R - Router, T - Trans Bridge, B - Source Route Bridge
                  S - Switch, H - Host, I - IGMP, r - Repeater, P - Phone
Device ID       Local Intrfce   Holdtme    Capability   Platform   Port ID
RR              Ser 0/0/0       128            R         C1841      Ser 0/0/1
LR              Ser 0/0/1       128            R         C1841      Ser 0/0/0
```

- On LR:
  1. Sh cdp neigh (Displays that MR is connected. It would be necessary to repeat the process to pass traffic thru MR to LR)

Point-to-Point Serial Connections:

There are multiple WAN technologies created to support networks which span extremely large geographic regions. A term often utilized in WAN topologies is "Point-to-Point Protocol (PPP)". PPP serial connections between routers often use a BUS topology or "end-to-end" series such as in the following illustration:

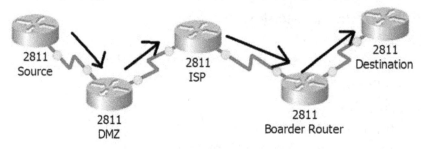

Bus Topology = Connected in Series one after another.

Each router is configured to communicate with directly connected neighbors. Early in the development of the Internet serial connections were used in this topology. With so many advances in both fiber optic and wireless communications basic PPP is becoming somewhat of a legacy system and is even being removed from specific Cisco and other network technology certification examination requirements. Although not a primary methodology utilized in many newer networks there are still many attributes which carry over into contemporary technologies. One of the aspects worth mentioning is the concept of "Encapsulation".

Encapsulation is the process of placing specific protocols and communications inside of encompassing protocols. This process is done for multiple reasons such as allowing communications to pass through devices which may not support a specific protocol, allowing maximization of convergence in routing topologies and sometimes creating methods of security to protect data contained within specific frames and packets. Some legacy configurations which still are inherent in contemporary communications include standards such as High-Level Data Link Control (HDLC) and Point-to-Point Protocol (PPP). For the sake of our discussion it is not necessarily to compare the two protocols but some of the following exercises will require the ability to configure either of them. To activate either protocol the following commands would be utilized:

- **Equipment to be used (Just Essentials):**
  - At least 2 Cisco Routers.
  - Associated cables for connections.

- **Encapsulation Configuration:**
  1. Config t
  2. (Conf)# int S0/0/0 (Selects the specific interface)
  3. (Config-if)#encap ppp (Activates protocol.)
     - OR: (Config-if)#encap hdlc (HDLC is the default on older routers.)

After activating either protocol the command "Sh int s0/0/0" could be utilized to confirm the setting. The topology above however, lends itself to the limitations of legacy bus topologies in the fact that there are too many points of failure. If "Boarder Router" fails, "Destination" no longer has Internet connections. Even worse, if "ISP" were to fail, the network is split in half with none having Internet access. To support network operations in the event that there is a single line of failure networks normally use a "RING" topology when designing WAN's such as illustrated below:

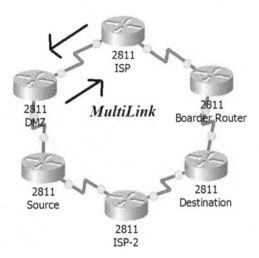

Notice in the RING topology there are two Internet Service Providers (ISP and ISP-2). Network communications can travel in two different directions. If any device were to fail, network services can still be sustained. At least four of the routers would have to fail simultaneously for this network to be adversely affected. Using this topology all of the locations have dedicated Internet access as well as the ability to reach other routers. Since there are two different paths for each device to reach one another communication protocols have to be enhanced to eliminate network congestion due to "hop-count" or tendency of the data to always use the same route of travel. For this reason in these typologies it is customary to use "Serial Multilink" methodologies. A multilink configuration allows the routers to always regard the source and destination to be directly connected although separated by other devices. So for example, if the message were to emanate from ISP-2 directed towards the DMZ router, a multilink protocol would configure the communications as if only those two routers exist regardless of the physical path of travel the messages take. An examples illustrated below:

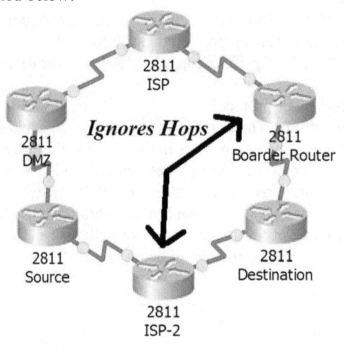

To illustrate configuring multilink serial connections the following commands are required. Note: The following commands are higher-level methods and may not be supported on many simulation software. To configure multilink the following commands would be utilized on all connected network interfaces:

1. (Config-if) #encap ppp (Interface may go down until both ends are configured)

2. (Config-if) # ppp multilink
3. (Config-if) # ppp multilink group 1

Authentication and Encapsulation:

The use of encapsulation in contemporary WAN configurations often support different types of authentication methods between routing devices. The authentication of devices requires the confirmation of identity prior to transmissions being accepted or allowed to flow through connected network devices. For example, when DMZ attempts to send a message to HQ the message must travel through ISP:

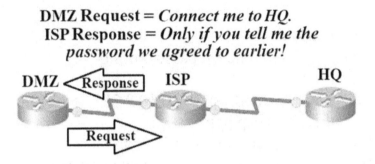

If DMZ does not provide the appropriate credentials all communications are discarded. Conversely, if the credentials are provided by DMZ then the communications are passed onto HQ but only if ISP also provides the credentials that HQ is expecting. The previous example is utilized by various security and authentication methods such as "Password Authentication Protocol (PAP)" and "Challenge Handshake Protocol (CHAP)". Both protocols authenticate communications between source and destinations but CHAP is often regarded as more secure due to its use of randomly generated strings of characters utilized in authentication processes. The following are examples of how either of the protocols could be configured on serial interfaces. **Note**: These activities are considered as higher-level network technology tasks and may not be supported on some simulation software.

- **Equipment to be used PPP with PAP (Just Essentials):**
    - o At least 2 Cisco routers (The 3rd will be assumed to be configured).
    - o Associated Serial cables for connections.

- **DMZ Configurations:**

1. DMZ(config)#username dmz password food (This is not a "person" but establishes a username for this router.)
2. DMZ(config)#int s0/0/0
3. DMZ(config-if)#ip address 10.10.10.1 255.255.255.0
4. DMZ(config-if)#clock rate 56000 (Establishes this interface as DCE.)
5. DMZ(config-if)#encap ppp
6. DMZ(config-if)#ppp authentication pap (Identifies authentication method.)
7. DMZ(config-if)#ppp pap sent-username isp password food (Specifies password "food" that will be expected by ISP router. I chose this password because I am presently hungry. LOL!)

- **ISP Configurations:**
  1. ISP(config)#username isp password food
  2. ISP(config)#int s0/0/1
  3. ISP(config-if)#ip address 10.10.10.2 255.255.255.0
  4. ISP(config-if)#encap ppp
  5. ISP(config-if)#ppp authentication pap
  6. ISP(config-if)#ppp pap sent-username dmz password food

At this stage all the configurations are established so communications will now pass between DMZ and ISP. When configuring serial interfaces remember it is required to establish DCE and DTE settings on connected interfaces between routing devices. To assure configurations for protocols as well as the interfaces the following commands are helpful:

- **show interface s0/0/#** = Display protocols and configuration information about specific interface.
- **show controllers s0/0/#** = To see which interface is the DTE or DCE.

Configuration for CHAP is very similar to the previous exercise with the addition that the username MUST BE identical to the hostname of the routing device. The process will be as follows:

- **Equipment to be used PPP with CHAP (Just Essentials):**
  - ➢ At least 2 Cisco routers (The 3rd will be assumed to be configured).
  - ➢ Associated Serial cables for connections.

- **DMZ Configurations:**

1. DMZ(config)#username isp password dog
2. DMZ(config)#interface s0/0/0
3. DMZ(config-if)#ip address 10.10.10.1 255.255.255.0
4. DMZ(config-if)#clock rate 56000
5. DMZ(config-if)#encapsulation ppp
6. DMZ(config-if)#ppp authentication chap (Specifies security method.)
7. DMZ(config-if)#no shut

- **ISP Configurations:**
    1. ISP_Router(config)#username isp password food
    2. ISP_Router(config)#int s0/0/1
    3. ISP(config)#username dmz password dog
    4. ISP(config)#interface s0/0/1
    5. ISP(config-if)#ip address 10.10.10.2 255.255.255.0
    6. ISP(config-if)#encapsulation ppp
    7. ISP(config-if)#ppp authentication chap
    8. ISP(config-if)#no shut

Just as in the earlier exercise, all the configurations are established so communications will now pass between DMZ and ISP. To assure configurations for protocols as well as the interfaces the following commands are helpful:

- **show interface s0/0/#** = Display protocols and configuration information about specific interface.
- **show controllers s0/0/#** = To see which interface is the DTE or DCE.

Chapter 13
Network Routing Elements

Network Routing Elements:

In quick review of what was previously mentioned about routers, routers have absolutely no settings on them when they are brand new. They also will not route any traffic upon turning them on. Every route, pathway and access rule required on a router has to be manually initiated by a network technician. The command set used for routers is similar to those of a Switch with a few additional parameters. Later in this text, there are examples on utilizing the elements below to initiate communications between and thru routers. The following are some of the settings required on a router.

- **Exit interface** = In a path statement, a router can be instructed in order to reach a non-connected network, send the packets out of an interface which is part of the router on which the command is being implemented. The advantage of this method is that the router has no need of knowing the ip address of where the packet is going. The possibility of typing in an incorrect ip for the other network device will not occur and the cpu does not have to utilize any time testing the IP address of the other network prior to sending the packet. This method, however, is somewhat insecure because the device connected to the other end of the routers connection could be changed at any time and the sending router will be unaware of the change, continuing to transmit packets out of the interface as long as there is a device attached to the other end of the cable.

- **Target interface** = In a pathway statement, this would be the IP address on the interface of the connected device which will know how to continue directing the packet towards its appropriate destination. Target interfaces are more secure because if the device on the other end of the cable is moved, the sending router will no longer route traffic to the device because the IP address is different than the IP address listed in the routing table. This method also however, increases CPU utilization because the router literally tests to see if the IP address matches prior to sending any packets to the destination IP address.

- **Routing Table** = This is a list of pathways the router can use to process traffic in order to send it to other networks. The entries in this table can be created manually or via utilizing protocols which communicate network path and conditions. Some methods are for smaller networks within a company while other methods are more widely used to allow traffic to travel over international connections (Internet for example).

- **Connected or "Local" Routes** = These are pathways displayed on a router due to cables being immediately attached to the router. Although the interfaces are connected, unless the port is configured, no traffic will pass thru the router.

- **Static Routes** = In order to route traffic to a network which is not directly connected it is necessary for a technician to manually input statements into the router. This method uses a "relay race" concept in which the statement tells the router, "In order to get to the router named "Destination", send the traffic through "R2". After R2 gets the transmission it is configured to reach "Destination" by sending the transmission to "R6" to allow the reception of data at "Destination".

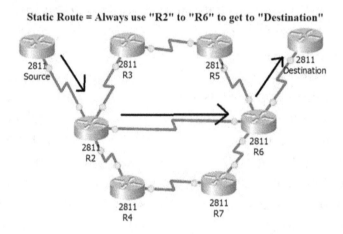

Static Route = Always use "R2" to "R6" to get to "Destination"

- **Default Route** = Much like a static route, the default route is more of a "catch all" or "if the network is unknown" entry. Essentially, a router uses this path if it has no statement which matches the destination of a packet. In this case, the Default Route directs unknown packets to another device with the idea that the other device will know how to find the requested unknown network.

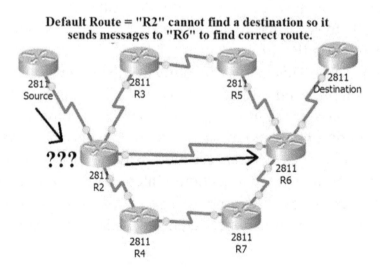

Default Route = "R2" cannot find a destination so it sends messages to "R6" to find correct route.

- **Summary Routes** = Multiple pathways on a router result in a number of possibilities in which could result in high CPU usage on the router. The more the router is processing pathways actually diminishes the speed of the router to pass packets to the appropriate destination. Using a special statement which compresses a number of paths into a single statement reduces processor load on the router due to the reduction of the number of paths the router evaluates. This process is called a "Summary Route". To create a summary route, all of the network paths must be similar in their octets going from left to right in "binary format". After finding the similarities between the leading numbers in the subnets, a new ip and netmask statement is created which includes the desired networks reducing the number of paths the router must evaluate prior to transmitting the packets. For greater clarity, exercises directly related to Summary Routes appear in the Lab exercises in this text.

Chapter 14
Dynamic Routing Protocols

Dynamic Routing Protocols:

The creation of static routing statements can become overwhelming to network administrators. Typos and miscommunications can easily result in a "black out" of sections of a network which supports no network communication until the system is repaired. In order to compensate for the nuances present in manual routing methods, there are options in which routers exchange information automatically about networks to which they have in their routing tables. This process results in all networks equipped with similar routing protocols to constantly maintain connections and pathways to networks as well as learning about other networks as soon as they become available. Dynamic Routing Protocols are often classified in the manner routers are determined and added to routing and topology tables. The following are two methods used by different Dynamic Routing Protocols:

- **Distance Vector** = Identifies the best path between source and destination based upon the shortest number of hops. If there are two paths, one with 10 hops and the other with 6 hops. Distance Vector will always select the "6-hop" path. This can become a problem if the shorter path is always congested, however. Data will be delayed or even lost in transmission due to timeout settings on receiving devices..
- **Link-State** = Evaluates multiple paths between source and destination and utilizes the route with the least congestion. This method allows fastest delivery of data but requires high CPU processing and RAM utilization on a router.

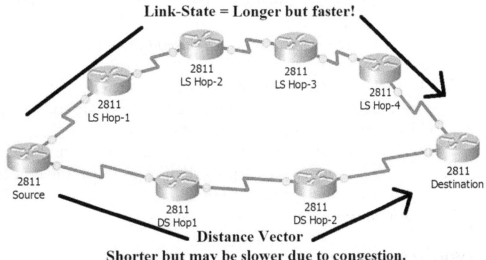

Shorter but may be slower due to congestion.

There is no best protocol to use in every situation and should be selected and configured due to the characteristics of the network (i.e., Number of devices, single location versus large multi-city environments, etc.) Some examples of dynamic routing protocols appear below:

- **RIP (Routing Internet Protocol)** = This is one of the older routing protocols which is not often used anymore. RIP allows the propagation of routing tables between connected neighbors. Some elements of RIP include;
  1. Utilizes "Distance Vector" method for path determination (Shortest distance is located and utilized). All other paths are disregarded. Maximum distance is 15 devices. Afterwards, the packets are dropped.
  2. Only understands Classfull address (Not CIDR\VLSM).
     ☐ Note: RIPv2 understands CIDR/VLSM.
  3. Sends updates every 30 seconds regardless of need.
  4. Uses broadcasts on 255.255.255.255 to update neighbor routing tables.
     ☐ Note: RIPv2 multicasts on 224.0.0.9.

- **EIGRP (Enhanced Interior Gateway Routing Protocol)** = This was originally a Cisco Propriety protocol which understands (CIDR) and VLSM. Other advantages are:
  1. Parallel links between sites with load balancing (If one line is congested, packets can use another. Only one route is advertised at any one time).
  2. Passwords and encryption can be used to validate routers allowed to update routing tables.
  3. Only sends updates when network routes are changed to enable convergence (Point in which all routing tables are equal).
  4. Only propagates tables between neighbors.
  5. Prefers neighbors although utilizes a "Link-State" protocol.
  6. Compatible with another legacy routing protocol called Interior Gateway Routing Protocol (IGRP).
  7. Multicasts on 224.0.0.10.

- **OSPF (Open Shortest Path First)** = This protocol uses a "Link-State" algorithm which attempts to isolate multiple paths between and thru interconnected networks in order to find the path which is the "Least

congested" regardless of the number of hops. Used in large enterprise networks, the following are some characteristics of OSPF:
1. Multicasts on 224.0.0.5 and 224.0.0.6
2. Has a Domain Router (DR) which maintains the authoritative map of the network) to which all routers report.
3. Utilizes a Backup Domain Router (BDR) in case the DR goes offline.

Wide Area Network (WAN) Traffic Routing:

After an IP's are placed on interfaces and electricity supplied, routers can only communicate with directly connected devices. In order for routers on extreme ends of network connections (Like those connected in "series") require configuration to allow them to communicate with devices to which they are separated from by one or more intermediate routing devices. In order to accomplish communications, routers need to possess a map of a network which would include sections of a network which are not directly connected. Take the following scenario:

In the above situation, LR can ping MR, MR can ping RR or LR and RR can ping MR. RR cannot communicate with LR however. Both RR and LR must be configured to communicate to one another thru MR. In order for communications to occur, both routers must have a "Routing Table" created. Routing tables are created in two manners:

- **Statically** = Manual entries are added to the router's running memory giving directions on how to reach connected networks.

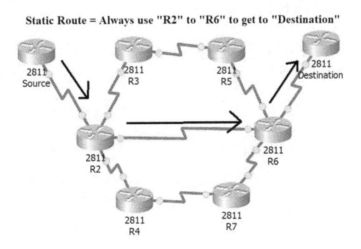

- **Dynamically** = Software (Protocols) in the routers operating systems are able to reach other routers and teach connected devices about other networks.

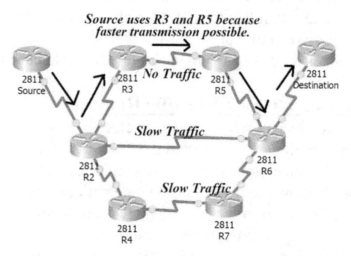

The following are methods in which routers can be manually configured for discontinuous (Not directly connected) networks or how the routers operating system can be setup to automatically learn about connected networks.

Administrative Distances and Values:

Routers can utilize multiple static and dynamic routing methods. There is the possibility that different routing methods are accidently directed to the same network location. Due to this, the routing table software on routers has the ability to select the most efficient method regardless of multiple entries and protocols on a router. Each method and protocol literally has a value as a default in routing tables. In Cisco router environments, the closer to the number "0", the more trusted the method (For example, the value of "1" is better than the value "2" or "3". The following are the values of some of the routing methods utilized in this text.

Routing Method Administrative Distances	
Route Source	Default Distance Values
Connected interface	0
Static route	1
Internal EIGRP	90
OSPF	110
Routing Information Protocol (RIP)	120
Exterior Gateway Protocol (EGP)	140

Chapter 15
Routing Table Concepts and Methods

Routing Table Concepts and Methods:

A routing table is the list or instructions of how a router knows where to send packets. Routers cannot locate any networks which are not directly connected to the local interfaces. In order to find other networks, the routers will utilize instructions referred to as a "Routing Table". The routing table can use various methods of routing including the following:

- **Static Route** = Manual entry which outlines paths between networks.
- **Dynamic Routes** = Routers possess protocols which allows routers to exchange routing tables automatically.
- **Default Route** = This is a statement in a routing table which is used when the router has packets for which there is no destination in the routing table. In this way, unknown destinations can be located by a different router.

The routing table can be created in any of the above ways. In the following exercises, we will utilize the methods listed in the following order, Static, Dynamic and then Default. The following exercises require the knowledge of the previous labs utilizing the routers indicated as "LR", "MR" and "RR". If they have not been completed, it is highly recommended that they are experienced prior to attempting the following labs.

Configuring a Static Route:

Perform the following exercises on routers "RR" "MR" and "LR":

- On LR:
  1. **Sh ip route** = This command displays all known networks and the pathways to get to them. You notice only the 172.16.20.y network is listed.

```
LR#sh ip route
Codes: C - connected, S - static, I - IGRP, R - RIP, M -
       D - EIGRP, EX - EIGRP external, O - OSPF, IA - OS
       N1 - OSPF NSSA external type 1, N2 - OSPF NSSA ex
       E1 - OSPF external type 1, E2 - OSPF external typ
       i - IS-IS, L1 - IS-IS level-1, L2 - IS-IS level-2
       * - candidate default, U - per-user static route,
       P - periodic downloaded static route

Gateway of last resort is not set

     172.16.0.0/24 is subnetted, 1 subnets
C       172.16.20.0 is directly connected, Serial0/0/0
```

- We need to teach LR to send packets to MR in order to get to RR. In order to allow communications between both networks, we need to update the routing table.
- In order to accomplish the routing, we can either use an "Exit Interface" or a "Target IP address". The following are examples of the two methods:

  2. **Target Interface** = With this process, we can tell the router if a packet arrives at the router destined for a particular destination, the packet should be forwarded to a specific IP on the network and that device will know how to route the packet. Using target interfaces are the more secure method although it increases the processing overhead on the router itself. The statement needed would be as follows:
     - Conf-t
     - Ip route 172.16.30.0 255.255.255.0 172.16.20.2

```
LR#conf t
Enter configuration commands, one per line.  End with CNTL/Z.
LR(config)#ip route 172.16.30.0 255.255.255.0 172.16.20.2
```

  3. **Sh ip route** = Command now displays the method to be used to communicate with the 172.16.30.y network (Which is between MR and RR).

```
LR#sh ip route|
Codes: C - connected, S - static, I - IGRP, R - RIP, M
       D - EIGRP, EX - EIGRP external, O - OSPF, IA - C
       N1 - OSPF NSSA external type 1, N2 - OSPF NSSA e
       E1 - OSPF external type 1, E2 - OSPF external ty
       i - IS-IS, L1 - IS-IS level-1, L2 - IS-IS level-
       * - candidate default, U - per-user static route
       P - periodic downloaded static route

Gateway of last resort is not set

     172.16.0.0/24 is subnetted, 2 subnets
C       172.16.20.0 is directly connected, Serial0/0/0
S       172.16.30.0 [1/0] via 172.16.20.2
```

- This is only half of the process. We also need a matching statement on RR to allow it to locate LR or the 172.16.20.y network. Login to RR and perform the remaining commands:
    4. Conf t
    5. Ip route 172.16.20.0 255.255.255.0 172.16.30.1
    6. **Sh ip route** (Now RR displays the commands to get to LR. Now ping 172.16.20.1. The first attempt will render three out of 5. Repeat the ping and the 2nd time there should be 5 exclamation points.)
- **Exit interface** = This method concentrates on using the local interfaces on the router of which we are typing in the routing statements. The advantages of this method include reducing CPU computation for there is no attempt to check the next hop device. There is also no need to know the next hop's IP address. The disadvantage of this method includes that there is no confirming the security of the next hop prior to routing information to it. A hacker could replace the assumed next hop device with a fraudulent device which will pass traffic but capture and store any secret data for later harvesting. The following commands would be completing the static routing process using only "Exit" interfaces:

    7. Complete the following on LR:
        ➢ Conf-t
        ➢ **Ip route 172.16.30.0 255.255.255.0 s0/0** (This is the local interface of LR)
        ➢ **Sh ip route** (Command now displays the method to be used to communicate with the 172.16.30.y network (Which is between MR and RR)).
            ☐ This is only half of the process. We also need a matching statement on RR to allow it to locate LR or the 172.16.20.y network.
    8. Login to RR and perform the remaining commands:
        ➢ Conf t
        ➢ Ip route 172.106.20.0 255.255.255.0 s0/1
        ➢ Sh ip route (Now RR displays the commands to get to LR. Now ping 172.16.20.1. The first attempt will render three out of 5. Repeat the ping and the 2nd time there should be 5 exclamation points.)

Configuring a Default Route:

In the previous exercise, we configured communications between LR and RR. If we connect an additional router to either LR or RR we would have to repeat the previous activities of creating more routing statements. This can create a large routing table. In addition, there can be routes which are accidently missed. To control for missed networks, "Default Routes" are often used. A "Default Route" is a "catch-other" method. It simply instructs the router that if it encounters any packets of which it has no matching routes, the packet should be directed to another router which will know how to process the remainder of the packets direction. The process of creating a default route is identical to that of creating a static route as in the following:

- **Ip route 0.0.0.0 0.0.0.0 s0/1 (Or IP address of the target interface of another router)** = This is the normal process of instructing the router to use an exit interface or the identity of the network interface of a router which would be able to continue routing of the packets).

Configuring a "Backup" Default Route:

A primary concern in network communications is the existence of redundancy (Multiple methods to support identical operations in case the primary method fails). Routing tables use the "Default route" for redundancy in case the routing table does not have a matching entry. What happens when the "Default-Route" is not operating, however? In order to control for a failed default route, it is possible to create multiple backup default routes in case the primary route is non-functioning. The backup for the default route is often called a "Floating Default". This is done by identifying an additional network interface which can be used for traffic and manually assigning the additional default route a "Higher Distance Value". In "Cisco world", the further a number is from "0" the less desirable the route is compared to other routes. For example, the number "2" is better than the number "10". All routes in a routing table have a distance value. The distance value for any connected network is "0". All default routes have a distance value of "1". Specifics for values and distances will be discussed later in this chapter but let us concentrate on utilization of the backup default route. Below is a mini-lab which illustrates the process of a backup default route. In order to complete the following lab, you must recreate the previous "3 Router" lab:

- ON MR:
    - 9. **Sh ip route** (Will list all the connected networks as well as the default route we setup for s0/0/0.)

10. Sh run (Towards the bottom, you will see the default route also listed.)
11. Let's create a backup route:
    - ☐ Conf t
    - ☐ **Ip route 0.0.0.0 0.0.0.0 s0/0/1 5** (That last number "5" makes this route the backup).
    - ☐ End <enter>
12. Sh run (Notice that the new route appears with the previous default route.)
13. Sh ip route (Notice the new route does not appear.)
14. Either "Shut down" or temporarily disconnect s0/0/0.
15. "**Sh ip int brief** (Now you notice the backup default route appears in the routing table.)
16. Enable the connection on s0/0/0 before you continue with the labs in this book.

Route Summarization (Also called "Route Aggregation"):

Many routers have the ability to connect to multiple networks. The path which is utilized is called a "Routing Table". This table can have hundreds of lines which requires a large amount of processer utilization. The smaller a routing table, the more efficient a router will operate. If it is possible to reduce the size of a routers routing table the more effective the router will be concerning passing data to other networks. An available method to reducing routing tables is by using a "Summary Route". A "Summary route" uses a single statement to reflect multiple routes. The advantage is less processing and reduction in static routing statements required to reach remote networks. In the following example, in order to allow traffic to flow to all of the networks, the following routing statements would be required on the router listed as "ISP Connection" to reach the other networks:

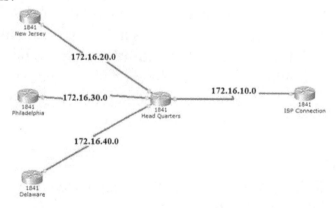

- Normally required routing statements on ISP connection:

> Ip route 172.16.20.0 255.255.255.0 S0/0
> Ip route 172.16.30.0 255.255.255.0 S0/0
> Ip route 172.16.40.0 255.255.255.0 S0/0

The above example includes only four networks. Functional networks often include hundreds of subnetworks. It would become overwhelming to manually type in all the entries. In addition, multiple routes require the router to use more processing time to confirm routes which can slowdown the transfer of packets. With a summary route, it is possible to compress all the networks into a smaller routing statement. In order to accomplish this, it is necessary to convert the network ID's and subnet masks into their binary representations. Using "binary representation", the routers combine all the routes into a single network statement which is then displayed in decimal format. The following is the process which would be used to create a summary route for the network illustrated below. (Note: The network 172.16.10.0 is not included because it is directly connected to ISP connection):

- **List all networks and convert to binary:**
  - 172.16.20.0 = 10101100.00010000.00010100.00000000
  - 172.16.30.0 = 10101100.00010000.00011110.00000000
  - 172.16.40.0 = 10101100.00010000.00101000.00000000
    - Notice that the first 18 bits in all of the subnets are identical when listed above each one another. The remaining bits are different.
- **Create a new 32-bit string, but change identical areas to binary "1's" while unmatching are "0's":**
  - 11111111.11111111.11000000.00000000
- **Convert binary string to new decimal subnet mask:**
  - 255.255.192.0
- **Identify sections of all networks with completely common octets:**
  - 172.16.10.0
  - 172.16.20.0
  - 172.16.30.0
  - 172.16.40.0
- **Create a new network statement from the common network octets:**
  - 172.16.0.0

- **Create new network statement which summarizes all networks included:**

- Summarized network = 172.16.0.0
- **Create new subnet mask statement which summarizes all networks included:**
  - Summarized Subnet = 255.255.192.0
- **IP route Summarization command:**
  - ip route 172.16.0.0 255.255.192.0 s0/0

Using this summarized command, it is now possible to reach all of the networks with a single routing statement. In addition, if any new networks are created within the range of the summary route, it will be automatically included. Any networks "higher" than the included summary route will have to be added with an additional routing statement or a new summary route statement will have to be included.

Chapter 16
Configuring Dynamic Routing Protocols

Configuring Dynamic Routing Protocols:

In most network infrastructures, there are multiple routers connected to multiple routers. The internet is the world's largest example of a network infrastructure with thousands of routers all over the world. There are new networks created almost every day. It would be an impossible task to attempt to update connected routers every time a new route appears or an old route is no longer functional. To control for maintaining a stable and up-to-date routing table on connected routers, special protocols are used to allow groups of routers to automatically compare and exchange routing table data to maintain a consistent and valid listing of all associated networks and the best paths to use to transfer data to them. When routers have the ability to exchange routing tables, they are said to be using "Dynamic Routing Protocols". Some Dynamic Routing Protocols are the following:

- **RIP (Routing Internet Protocol)** = Very old routing method primarily used in smaller networks but occasionally found still operating on some routers which need to communicate with older networks.
- **EIGRP (Enhanced Interior Gateway Routing Protocol)** = Used in mid-size and internal business networks.
- **OSPF (Open Shortest Path First)** = Often used in large network infrastructures or sections of the internet.
- **BGP (Boarder Gateway Protocol)** = Often used between large disconnected network infrastructures on the internet.

Routes can use both static, default and dynamic routes simultaneously. The router will select active routes based on the values and distances listed for specific methods and protocols. Below is a chart which identifies the values and distances of some routing protocol methods:

Routing Method Administrative Distances	
Route Source	Default Distance Values
Connected interface	0
Static route	1
Internal EIGRP	90
OSPF	110
Routing Information Protocol (RIP)	120
Exterior Gateway Protocol (EGP)	140

The following labs allow the utilization of EIGRP, OSPF and BGP. Before attempting the labs, it is highly recommended that all previous labs have been completed. In addition, we will be using the same network as in the section for "Static Routing" removing some of the commands used in the earlier project:

EIGRP Configuration Exercise:

The routing table can be created in any of the above ways. In the following exercise, we will utilize EIGRP dynamic routing. The following exercises require the knowledge of the previous labs utilizing the routers indicated as "LR", "MR" and "RR". If they have not been completed, it is highly recommended that they are experience prior to attempting the following labs.

17. On LR, execute the following commands:
    - ☐ Sh ip route = Notice that the router only shows the local connected routes.
    - ☐ Conf t
    - ☐ **IP classless** = This command ensures that the routers will propagate correct subnet mask information with network settings. In addition, it allows the router to understand both Classfull and CIDR routing.
    - ☐ **Router eigrp 10** = Engages the EIGRP protocol and associates it with a process ID of "10" for the router.
    - ☐ **Network 172.16.20.0 0.0.0.255** = Establishes the network information the protocol with propagate to other routers. It also includes an "Inverse Subnet Mask (Sometimes called a "Wildcard Mask)". Essentially, this is the subnet mask for the network subtracted from 255.255.255.255.
    - ☐ End <enter>
    - ☐ **sh ip protocol** = This command is used to display any routing protocols presently enabled on a router. You will notice that EIGRP is now listed.

18. On MR execute the following commands:
    - ☐ Sh ip route = Notice that the router only shows the local connected routes.
    - ☐ Conf t
    - ☐ IP classless
    - ☐ Router eigrp 10
    - ☐ Network 172.16.30.0 0.0.0.255
    - ☐ Network 172.16.20.0 0.0.0.255
    - ☐ End
        - ➢ Soon after you type "end" you will notice "Adjacency Found" messages on your terminal. This means that a neighboring router is exchanging routing table information with this LR.

```
%DUAL-5-NBRCHANGE: IP-EIGRP 10:
 Neighbor 172.16.20.2 (Serial0/1/1) is up: new adjacency
```

- Sh ip route = EIGRP routes are now listed preceded by the letter "D". Listed now are the routes known by MR. Connect to LR and look at the routes.
19. On LR:
   - Sh ip route = EIGRP routes on MR are now listed. Let's now connect RR.
20. On RR:
   - Conf t
   - IP classless
   - Router eigrp 10
   - Network 172.16.40.0 0.0.0.255
   - Network 172.16.30.0 0.0.0.255
   - End
   - Sh ip route = Now RR knows all routes connected to both LR and MR.
   - Ping all interfaces which lead up to LR and you will get 100%.

- Dynamic Routing protocols can also allow default routes to be propagated to other routing devices so there will be no need to manually input the route on connected neighbors. In order to simulate the process, we will temporarily connect a PC to LR FastEthernet interface. The following process is used to teach EIGRP to use and propagate default routes:
21. On LR:
   - Conf t
   - Int fa0/0
   - Ip add 172.16.90.1 255.255.255.0 (This IP will lead to the PC)
   - No shut
   - End
   - Sh ip int brief = This will display S0/0/0 "up" and "up" but the Fa0/0 "down" and "up" because it has electricity flowing but no IP address. This will be fine for our lab.
   - Conf t
   - **Ip route 0.0.0.0 .0.0.0.0 fa0/0** = Establishes a default route which directs unknown packets to fa0/0.
   - End

☐ Sh ip route = You now see the Default Route listed with an asterisk (*). Let's continue to make it available for all routers.

```
Gateway of last resort is 0.0.0.0 to network 0.0.0.0
     172.16.0.0/16 is variably subnetted, 7 subnets, 6 masks
D       172.16.20.0/24 [90/2172416] via 172.16.30.2, 00:11:39, Serial0/0/0
D       172.16.30.0/24 [90/2172416] via 172.16.40.2, 00:11:39, Serial0/0/1
D       172.16.40.0/24 [90/2172416] via 172.16.50.2, 00:11:35, Serial0/1/0
S*   0.0.0.0/0 is directly connected, Serial0/0/0
LR#
```

☐ Conf t

☐ **Redistribute Static** = Command inserts the static route into EIGRP to transmit to connected neighbors.

☐ End

☐ Sh run = Towards the bottom you will see the routing statements for EIGRP including the redistribute static command.

```
router eigrp 10
 redistribute static
 network 172.16.30.0 0.0.0.255
 network 172.16.40.0 0.0.0.255
 network 172.16.50.0 0.0.0.255
 auto-summary
!
```

☐ Log onto MR and evaluate the routes.

22. On MR:

☐ Sh ip route = Now includes a statement of a default route listed with a "D" and an asterisk (*) indicating it is a default route learned via EIGRP. Go to RR and evaluate the routing table:

23. On RR:

☐ Sh ip route = Displays all networks and the default route leading to LR thru MR:

☐ **EIGRP Debug commands** = Can be used to confirm EIGRP configurations and communications. Please note, the commands will result in continued updates to the terminal interface. You must be able to swiftly type commands in full between updates or your commands will be ignored on the router. In order to disable the commands listed,…type the word "No" in front of the command used to enable to feature:

➤ **Debug IP Pack** = This command will display messages when packets include the IP address being multicast from the router.

The multicast 224.0.0.10 is one of the indicators of participating in an EIGRP environment.

> **Debug eigrp pack** = This will only display communications concerning EIGRP transmissions. Other IP packets will be ignored.

OSPF Configuration Exercise:

The routing table can be created in any of the above ways. In the following exercise, we will utilize OSPF dynamic routing. The following exercises require the knowledge of the previous labs utilizing the routers indicated as "LR", "MR" and "RR". If they have not been completed, it is highly recommended that they are experienced prior to attempting the following labs. The following process is used to teach OSPF to use and propagate default routes. In this lab, we will connect each router to one another in a closed loop. We will modify the design by renaming the routers as following:

24. LR = R1
25. MR = R2
26. RR = R3
27. Connect the s0/0 on R3 to the S0/1 on R1. Establish this as the 172.16.40.0 network. Make either end the DCE.
28. On R1:
    - ☐ Conf t
    - ☐ IP classless
    - ☐ **Router OSPF 10**
    - ☐ **Network 172.16.20.0 0.0.0.255 area 0** = OSPF requires an "Area Number" which would allow the grouping of specific interfaces which would exclusively exchange routing table information. In this scenario, we have selected the area number "0".
    - ☐ Network 172.16.40.0 0.0.0.255 area 0 = This network will be finished last connecting to R3.
    - ☐ End
    - ☐ Sh run = Look for routing statements at bottom of display. No changes or routes will display in table because R1 is the only router participating in OSPF at this time. Go to R2 and perform the following:
29. On R2:
    - ☐ Conf t
    - ☐ IP classless
    - ☐ Router OSPF 10

☐ Network 172.16.20.0 0.0.0.255 area 0
☐ Network 172.16.30.0 0.0.0.255 area 0
☐ End = The Terminal will start displaying "New Adjacency"
☐ Sh IP route = Displays all networks which have OSPF enabled. Complete the network on R3:

30. On R3:
☐ Conf t
☐ IP classless
☐ Router OSPF 10
☐ Network 172.16.30.0 0.0.0.255 area 0
☐ Network 172.16.40.0 0.0.0.255 area 0
☐ End = The Terminal will start displaying "New Adjacency"
☐ Sh IP route = Displays all OSPF networks.
☐ Ping to any network interface successfully!

31. **OSPF Default Routes** = Just like the previous protocol, OSPF can also be used to propagate the existence of a default route to routers participating in the same area. We must connect and turn on one of the FA0/0 interfaces on R1 and connect it to a computer.

32. On R1:
☐ Sh IP route = Displays all the routes learned by OSPF.
☐ Conf t
☐ Int fa0/0
☐ Ip add 172.16.80.1 255.255.255.0
☐ No shut
☐ IP route 0.0.0.0 0.0.0.0 fa0/0
☐ End
☐ Conf t
☐ **OSPF 10**
☐ **Default-information originate** = This command orders OSPF neighbors to use the default route on R1.
☐ Sh ip route = Displays the OSPF routes and the Default Route.
☐ Sh run = Towards the bottom it is indicated that OSPF will be propagating the default route. Now let's go to R2.

33. On R3:

☐ Sh ip route = Displays a "O" route with an "E*" indicating it as a static route propagated by OSPF.

34. **OSPF Helping commands** = Can be used to confirm OSPF configurations and communications. Please note, the commands will result in continued updates to the terminal interface. You must be able to swiftly type commands in full between updates or your commands will be ignored on the router. In order to disable the commands listed, type the word "No" in front of the command used to enable to feature:

> **Debug IP Pack** = This command will display messages within packets including the IP address being multicast from the router. The multicast 224.0.0.5 is one of the indicators of participating in an OSPF environment.

> **Sh ip ospf neigh** = Displays all connected routers using OSPF including IP address and specific network connections.

> **debug ip ospf events** = Displays processes related to OSPF updates, communications, keep-alives, etc.

Advanced OSPF Configurations:

OSPF is another dynamic routing protocol which is used in larger networks to propagate routing tables. OSPF operates by organizing sections of networks into areas. For routing purposes these areas are essentially a collection of routing devices that share common media such as cables or wireless SSID's. The organized devices are part of an OSPF Domain supporting the transmission of data which is classified as an "AS (Autonomous System)" utilized to allow the devices within the area to communicate with one another.   All of the devices within the area maintain an identical routing table for networks and subnets. The process of tables being propagated and updated to a consistent condition is called "Convergence".

OSPF uses paths of communication determined based upon "Adjacencies (Confirmed active links between directly connected routers). The adjacencies includes both directly connected and remote networks separated by a series of devices. Once determined, the OSPF routers ignore the fact that multiple hops may exist between source and destination and regard each path as a single connection. OSPF routing tables may contain multiple active paths between sources and destinations. OSPF is classified as a "Link-State" protocol because it determines the best communication path based upon available bandwidth compared to congestion on known routes between sources and destinations. Some well-known features of OSPF would include the following:

- No limit to how many devices can be included in the path between source and destination.
- Supports VLSM (Variable-Length Subnet Masks).
- Supports multiple paths to identical destinations.

An important aspect of OSPF is how routing tables are contained and propagated. The protocol utilizes identities on routing devices indicating their purpose in the area. The following are some of the designations which can be found in an OSPF topography:

- **Designated Router (DR)** = This router is the most essential router in OSPF operations. The DR maintains the most up to date routing topology to any known networks.
- **Backup Designated Router (BDR)** = This router also contains a master topology table which becomes active if the DR stops operating.
- **Designated Router Other (DROther)** = These are routers in the OSPF environment which are participating but do not serve as either DR or BDR,

Once paths are determined a topology map is developed on at least one router classified as the "Designated Router (DR) and then prorogated to other routers in the same area. Any changes to the area are also reported back to the DR which alters the topology resulting in the DR changing its master tables and once again propagating the new tables to all routers participating in the area.

One of the areas often mentioned within OSPF discussions is a "backbone" section. This is a logical collection of participating devices regarded as the base or foundation of the OSPF topology. Traditionally this area is identified as "area 0" and normally serves as the bridge between multiple separated networks. The benefit of the backbone area is the segmenting of different topologies to reduce the size of routing tables, reduce the time of convergence (Process of updating all routing tables), as well as diminishing transference of various redundant and possibly incorrect routing paths.

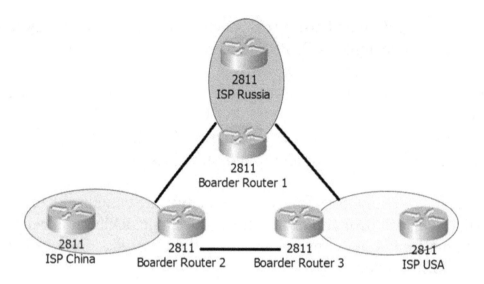

There are many configurations available with OSPF. The litany of configurations are broad and exceed the expectations of this text but the following are few examples:

- **Point to Point** = When a single interface on least two different network devices are directly connected to one another.

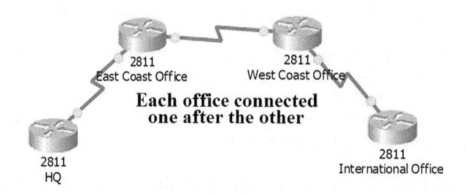

- **Non-Broadcast Multiaccess (NBMA)** = Allows the manual determination of the Designated Router (DR) and Backup Designated Router (BDR).

OSPF Broadcast Multi-Access Environments

Multi-access OSPF areas exists when a single communication media is connected to multiple network devices. This could be in the case in which multiple routers are connected to a series of Layer 3 Switches (Performs as both a Router and a Switch) or participate in the same SSID. OSPF uses broadcasts to update and propagate topography information to be used throughout the area. In order to exchange routing tables OSPF uses "Link State Advertisements (LSA)" to communicate the existence of connected networks. If any aspect of a OSPF connection alters (i.e., Bandwidth, Congestion, Disconnection, etc.) in any way it triggers immediate broadcast of LSA updates. Although very effective, if misconfigured this can result in multiple redundant adjacencies which could actually reduce the functionality of the network.

Because the nature of routing devices there are always fluctuations in availability. To reduce the likelihood of broadcast storms OSPF have configuration options called "Election" which can streamline the exchange of routing tables. This allows topology updates to emanate from a single router as opposed to every router in the network. During an election the routing protocol determines the ultimate routing table authority in the AS. Once the election is concluded there will be one router classified as a "Designated Router (DR)". This router in the area holds the master topology table which is propagated other routers within the OSPF AS. In addition, for redundancy purposes there will also be a "Backup Designated Router (BDR)" which also holds a master copy of the topology. The BDR becomes the primary authority for routing topologies if the DR cannot be contacted. Any other routers participating in the OSPF AS are classified as "Designated Other Routers (DROthers)" and receive their topology information from either the DR or the BDR.

OSPF Elections:

When discussing OSPF there is value in understanding the election process. OSPF has mechanisms within the protocol to attempt a determination of which devices should be the DR, BDR or DROthers. The process utilizes various options from the following in order from first to last:

- **Highest Connected Network Interface IP Address in the OSPF Area =** This would be the actual IP address used on a physical interface. This is the default in OSPF elections. It is not best practice to rely on IP's in OSPF elections due to potential equipment changes on networks such as failed interfaces and changing IP addresses. A router in an office not essential in a network could also become the DR as in the illustration below:

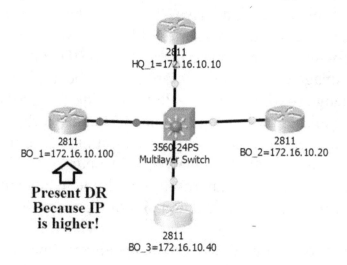

- **OSPF Priority** = This is a manual configuration performed on a router using the "ip ospf priority <0-255>" command. If this method is used the router with the highest number becomes the DR and the second highest is the BDR. The default for priority settings is "1". If the configured priority number is "0" the router is prohibited from being a DR in any election. If any two routers have the same priority number ("Tie") then a DR is wins an election by using a "Router ID".
- **Router ID** = This is a manual configuration performed on the router using the "router-id 0.0.0.0" command. Notice the command includes a statement which looks similar to an IP address. These four digits do not participate in any type of communications and is purely for OSPF election processes. In this method, the mathematically highest router-ID becomes the DR and the next is the BDR.
- **Loopback Interface** = This is a manual configuration performed on the router creating a "virtual" network interface using the "Interface Loopback <n>" command followed by the "ip add n.n.n.n s.s.s.s" command. The command is identical to configuring a physical network interface. This setting allows both OSPF participation and remote management such as telnet and SSH.

NOTE: It is normally suggested that only one of the above options are utilized. Combining the above methods often cause complications and resultant election or convergence problems.

Configuring OSPF Election:

The following are examples of how to configure OSPF using the different discussed methods. All scenarios start with the DR configured automatically from the IP address election. All scenarios will use an identical topology with the desire to move the DR to the "HQ_1" router as illustrated below:

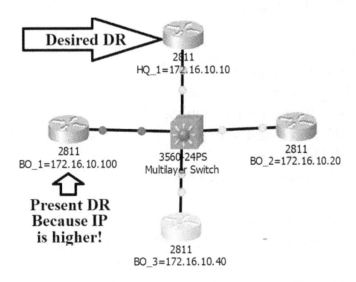

- **Equipment to be used:**
  o Four Routers
  o Single Switch connecting Routers.

- **OSFP LoopBack Setup:**
  ➢ **HQ_1 (Desired Designated Router):**
  1. HQ_1(config)#router ospf 5
  2. HQ_1(config)#network 172.16.10.0 0.0.0.255 area 0
  3. HQ_1(config)#int loopback 0 (Activates loopback interface)
  4. HQ_1(config-if)#ip add 4.4.4.4 255.255.255.255 (This will be the highest interface number making this unit the DR)
  5. HQ_1(config-if)#exit

  ➢ **BO_1 (Desired Backup Designated Router:**
  1. BO_1(config)#router ospf 5
  2. BO_1(config)#network 172.16.10.0 0.0.0.255 area 0
  3. BO_1(config)#int loopback 0
  4. BO_1(config-if)#ip add 3.3.3.3 255.255.255.255 (Will be BDR)
  5. BO_1(config-if)#exit

  ➢ **BO_2:**

1. BO_2(config)#router ospf 5
2. BO_2(config)#network 172.16.10.0 0.0.0.255 area 0
3. BO_2(config)#int loopback 0
4. BO_2(config-if)#ip add 2.2.2.2 255.255.255.255 (Will be DROther)
5. BO_2(config-if)#exit

➢ **BO_3:**
1. BO_3(config)#router ospf 5
2. BO_3(config)#network 172.16.10.0 0.0.0.255 area 0
3. BO_3(config)#int loopback 0
4. BO_3(config-if)#ip add 1.1.1.1 255.255.255.255 (Will be DROther)
5. BO_3(config-if)#exit

After configuring all of the routers there is now the need to update all topology tables with a "Re-election" activated with the "Router#clear ip ospf process" command. After typing the command a confirmation will appear displayed as **"Reset ALL OSPF processes? [no]: yes"**. Enter "yes" and the re-election will start. Perform the command on EVERY ROUTER and look for the **"%OSPF-5-ADJCHG: Process 5, Nbr 0.0.0.12 on FastEthernet0/0 from LOADING to FULL, Loading Done"** notices. After the re-election there are a few commands which can be used to verify connectivity such as the following:

- **sh ip ospf neigh** = Displays connected OSPF Routers and Status.
- **Sh ip route ospf** = Displays OSPF routing Tables.
- **Sh ip prot** = Displays all running routing protocols.

NOTE: Sometimes you will see **"EXSTART"** or **"2Way"** when election processes are underway.

- **OSFP Priority ID Setup:**
  ➢ **HQ_1:**
  1. HQ_1(config)#router ospf 5
  2. HQ_1(config)#network 172.16.10.0 0.0.0.255 area 0
  3. HQ_1(config)#interface gi0/0
  4. HQ_1(config-if)#ip ospf priority 100 (Will be DR)
  5. HQ_1(config -if)#exit

  ➢ **BO_1:**

1. BO_1(config)#router ospf 5
2. BO_1(config)#network 172.16.10.0 0.0.0.255 area 0
3. BO_1(config)#interface gi0/0
4. BO_1(config-if)#ip ospf priority 50 (Will be BDR)
5. BO_1(config -if)#exit

> **BO _2:**
  1. BO_2(config)#router ospf 5
  2. BO_2(config)#network 172.16.10.0 0.0.0.255 area 0
  3. BO_2(config)#interface gi0/0
  4. BO_2(config-if)#ip ospf priority 40 (Will be DROther)
  5. BO_2(config -if)#exit

> **BO _3:**
  1. BO_3 (config)#router ospf 5
  2. BO_3(config)#network 172.16.10.0 0.0.0.255 area 0
  3. BO_3 (config)#interface gi0/0
  4. BO_3 (config-if)#ip ospf priority 30 (Will be DROther)
  5. BO_3 (config -if)#exit

After configurations, remember to use the **"Router#clear ip ospf process"** for the re-election and the verification commands to assure correct DR and BDR assignment.

- **OSFP Router ID Setup:**
  > **HQ_1:**
    1. HQ_1(config)#router ospf 5
    2. HQ_1(config)#network 172.16.10.0 0.0.0.255 area 0
    3. HQ_1(config)#router-id 0.0.0.100 (Will be DR)
    4. HQ_1(config -if)#exit

  > **BO_1:**
    1. BO_1(config)#router ospf 5
    2. BO_1(config)#network 172.16.10.0 0.0.0.255 area 0
    3. BO_1(config)# router-id 0.0.0.50 (Will be BDR)
    4. BO_1(config-if)#exit

  > **BO_2:**
    1. BO_2(config)#router ospf 5
    2. BO_2(config)#network 172.16.10.0 0.0.0.255 area 0
    3. BO_2(config)#router-id 0.0.0.30
    4. BO_2(config -if)#exit

> **BO_3:**
1. BO_3(config)#router ospf 5
2. BO_3(config)#network 172.16.10.0 0.0.0.255 area 0
3. BO_3(config)#router-id 0.0.0.20
4. BO_3(config -if)#exit

After configurations, remember to use the "Router#clear ip ospf process" for the re-election and the verification commands to assure correct DR and BDR assignment.

BGP (Border Gateway Protocol) Configuration Exercise:

Communicating on the Internet there are an overwhelming number of different Internet Service Providers, public and private networks and connected devices. Having one simple protocol to support all the networking functions required on the Internet would be a problematic enterprise. To support the interconnectedness of so many different networks it is required to utilize a very robust and multiplatform protocol which allows communications but at the same time does not overwhelm the routing tables used to direct traffic. One of the major protocols used on the Internet is classified as "Border Gateway Protocol (BGP)". This protocol is utilized on many major routers on the Internet maintained by the Department of Defense and many Internet Service Providers. BGP allows communication and exchanging of routing tables between specific routers without requiring full exchange of all traffic routes. This both reduces the number of entries existing on routing devices but also provides levels of security by allowing discrete networks to keep particular routes and networks unknown by their surrounding neighbors. A feature of BGP is the use of "Autonomous System Numbers (AS)". These allow specific routers to exchange routing information with other specific routers. Devices in the same AS are allowed to exchange routing information with one another while prohibiting devices who are not part of the same autonomous system. Internet Service Providers selectively pick routers on the "boarders" of their networks supporting communications between other separated networks. Another interesting aspect about BGP is it allows the routing tables to behave as if the distinct networks are adjacent to one another as opposed to being separated by large geographic distances. There are two types of BGP presently in use being classified as "internal" and "external". The nuances of the two different types are not particular to the discussion included in this text but the following will provide option for the configuration BGP. Please note, because BGP is a higher-order routing protocol it may not be supported in many routing simulation software. The following instructions are examples of commands utilized on actual Cisco routing equipment. We will be configuring four routers to support BGP between two discrete networks as illustrated below:

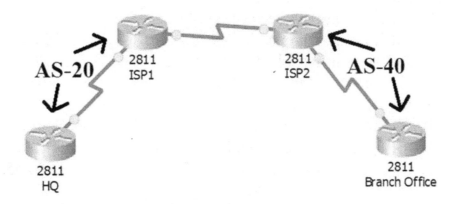

In this scenario there are two Internet Service providers who are connected through BGP. The connection is used by a company with two locations each connected to different Internet Service providers. When the Internet Service providers are established on the Internet to allow communications they must establish BGP connections with other Internet backbone routers. The following are the commands which could be utilized:

- **Equipment to be used:**
  - ○ At least four Cisco Routers with BGP functionality
  - ○ High-Speed Serial connections between each router (Can be done using Category connections).

- **BGP Setup:**
  - ➤ **HQ Router:**
    1. HQ(config)#int S0/0
    2. HQ(config-if)#ip address 172.16.20.1 255.255.255.0
    3. HQ(config-if)#Clock Rate 56000
    4. HQ(config-if)#no shutdown
    5. HQ(config)#router bgp 20 (Activates BGP autonomous system group)
    6. HQ(config-router)#neighbor 172.16.20.2 remote-as 20 (Identifies BGP partner)

  - ➤ **ISP 1 Router** (Note = ISP's routers will participate in two different AS groups. One between the ISP's and one for the connected private network):

1. ISP1(config)# int S0/1
2. ISP1(config)# int S0/1
3. ISP1(config-if)#ip address 172.16.20.2 255.255.255.0
4. ISP1(config-if)#no shutdown
5. ISP1(config-if)#interface int S0/0
6. ISP1(config-if)#ip address 172.16.30.1 255.255.255.0
7. ISP1(config-if)#Clock Rate 56000
8. ISP1(config-if)#no shutdown
9. ISP1(config)#router bgp 20
10. ISP1(config-router)#neighbor 172.16.20.1 remote-as 20
11. ISP1(config-router)#neighbor 172.16.30.2 remote-as 40
12. ISP1(config-router)#network 172.16.20.0 mask 255.255.255.0
    (Identifies AS network)
13. ISP1(config-router)#neighbor 172.16.20.1 next-hop-self
    (Identifies AS controller)

> **ISP 2 Router:**
1. ISP2(config)#int S0/1
2. ISP2(config-if)#ip address 172.16.30.2 255.255.255.0
3. ISP2(config-if)#no shutdown
4. ISP2(config-if)#int S0/0
5. ISP2(config-if)#ip address 172.16.40.1 255.255.255.0
6. ISP2(config-if)#Clock Rate 56000
7. ISP2(config-if)#no shutdown
8. ISP2(config)#router bgp 40
9. ISP2(config-router)#neighbor 172.16.40.2 remote-as 40
10. ISP2(config-router)#neighbor 172.16.30.1 remote-as 20
11. ISP2(config-router)#network 172.16.40.0 mask 255.255.255.0
12. ISP2(config-router)#neighbor 172.16.40.2 next-hop-self

> **Branch Office Router:**
1. BO(config)#int S0/1
2. BO(config-if)#ip address 172.16.40.2 255.255.255.0
3. BO(config-if)#no shutdown
4. BO(config)#router bgp 40
5. BO(config-router)#neighbor 172.16.40.1 remote-as 40

After configuring all of the routers there are a few commands which can be used to verify connectivity such as the following:
* **show ip bgp** = Displays Routes and peers.

- **show ip bgp summary** = Displays neighbors and route statistics.
- **show ip bgp neighbors** = Displays neighbors with IP settings.
- **show ip bgp rib-failure** = Displays routes which have not been loaded.

Chapter 17
Combining Router and Switch Technologies

Combining Router and Switch Technologies:

In most networks, routers and switches work together in order to allow access to resources as well as providing different levels of security. In the following labs, we will explore methods of configuring the services and functions of both routers and switches in scenarios similar to that of a small to mid-size network infrastructure. The following labs require the mastery of all previous labs. Many commands and equipment required in upcoming exercises will not be listed if they existed in previous labs. It is highly encouraged to complete all previous exercises before continuing.

- **Router-Switch-2PC's** = In this exercise, we will enable communications between router, a switch and two PC's. There will be a few optional commands listed which would not be required for the specific exercise but are "best practice" when configuring devices. For the exercise, the equipment will have the following configurations:
    - ☐ R1 = Fa0/0 with IP of 172.16.20.1 255.255.255.0
    - ☐ Connect R1's Fa0/0 to Switch 1's Fa0/1
    - ☐ Switch_1 = Int VLAN1 with IP of 172.16.20.2.
    - ☐ PC1 = IP of 172.16.20.10 255.255.255.0 and default gateway of 172.16.20.1
    - ☐ PC2 = IP of 172.16.20.20 255.255.255.0 and default gateway of 172.16.20.1
    - ☐ Connect the PC's to the any ports excluding ports 1 and 2 (Optional. These ports will be used for specific functions in upcoming labs).
    - ☐ On both PC's, ping the interface on the router.
    - ☐ On the terminal emulator, ping from Router to PC's.

    1. On R1:
    - ☐ **Sh cdp neigh** = This should display the Switch being connected.
    - ☐ Open a command line on both PC's and ping between each PC.

Dynamic Host Configuration Protocol on Routers:

There are a number of services that a router can provide to a network. One of those features is the ability to provide DHCP (Dynamic Host Configuration Protocol) services. The following lab gives instructions on the configuration for a DHCP-enabled router. Many requirements for the network will duplicate the settings used on previous labs. It is highly recommended that previous labs have been completed prior to beginning the following labs. For the exercise, the equipment will have the following configurations:

- R1 = Fa0/0 with IP of 172.16.20.1 255.255.255.0
- Connect R1's Fa0/0 to Switch_1's Fa0/1
- Switch_1 = Int VLAN1 with IP of 172.16.20.2.
- Connect the PC's to the any ports excluding ports 1 and 2 (Optional. These ports will be used for specific functions in upcoming labs).
- DHCP Process on R1:
  2. Conf t
  3. **Service DHCP** = This command enables/starts the service. Some routers will already have the service enabled by default.
  4. **ip dhcp pool name 1stDHCP** = This command creates a collection of IP settings. Many different groups of IP settings can be created on the same exact router. A group of IP settings is called a "Scope".
  5. **Network 172.16.20.0 255.255.255.0** = Command states that the IP range of 172.16.20.0 thru 172.16.20.255 will be distributed with an associated subnet mask of 255.255.255.0.
  6. **Default-router 172.16.20.1** = This supplies the default gateway setting for clients.
  7. **Lease 0 0 5** = This sets how much time the clients will be able to keep the dynamic IP settings. The syntax is in "Days-Hours-Minutes". We are setting this for only 5 minutes for lab purposes.
  8. **Domain-Name Cool.com** = This supplies the domain name setting for clients.
  9. **DNS-Server 172.16.10.10** = Establishes the Domain Name Server for network.
  10. **End**
  11. **Sh run** (You should now see the settings for DHCP towards the top of the readout. Now let us check to see if the PC's can get an IP address.)

- On PC1 = Open a command prompt.
  12. Type in the command "ipconfig /renew" (The readout will display the ip address given from the DHCP server along with the Default gateway and Subnet mask. You can also check which IP's the DHCP Router have distributed by doing the following on R1:
    ➤ **sh ip dhcp binding** (All devices which have been given an IP addresses along with their mac-address))

Router-on-a-Stick:

Many organizations have many separations within their networks. When this occurs, there is a need for different default gateway for each of the networks. In addition, these types of networks often have multiple VLANs reflective of different sections of the company. Often time, default gateways are individual routers connected to each network section.

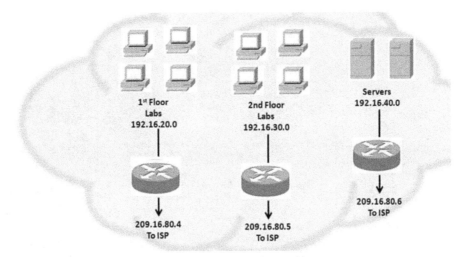

Unfortunately, routers are often extremely expensive and require large support staffs. A method to avoid multiple routers would be a single router with multiple interfaces each connecting to a separate subnet. Although not as expensive as the prior option, the multiple interfaces require a higher-powered router with additional slots.

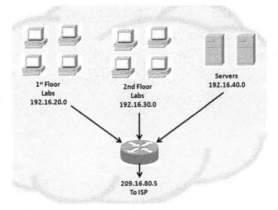

In order to require a lesser number of routers and smaller support staff, there is an option to customize a single router to support multiple networks with different IP schemes. Essentially, the router will use software to create many "simulated network interfaces" on a single real network interface. These simulated interfaces are called "Sub-Interfaces". When this method is utilized, the router must have a higher order processor and increased amount of RAM in order to support the amount of packets which will be routed internally on the router. A term which is often used to identify the existence of a single router with multiple simulated interfaces is called "Router-on-a-Stick." A representation is below:

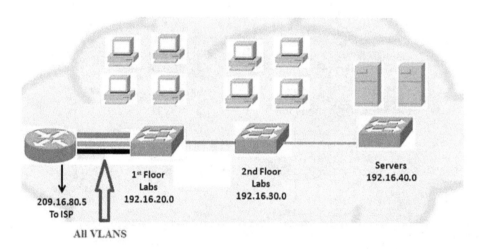

The process below outlines the process of configuring router on a stick. We will use the following loadout of equipment:

- Router "To ISP 209.16.80.5"
- 1st Floor Lab Switch = Int VLAN1 with IP of 192.16.20.2.
- Connect the PC's to the any ports excluding ports 1 and 2 (Optional. These ports will be used for specific functions in upcoming labs).
- Connect Router "To ISP" Fa0/0 to 1st Floor Lab Switch Fa0/1
- **On Router "To ISP** = We will create a "management" VLAN. This VLAN does not route traffic but primarily allows routers and switches to communicate. In addition, the computer station used by the Network Administrator is normally part of this VLAN to control and configure devices.
    13. Conf t
    14. Int fa0/0
    15. No shut = Enables interface without an IP address.
    16. Exit = will move you back to global configuration mode.
    17. **Int fa0/0.1** = The ".1" creates a sub-interface which the terminal indicates is active.
    18. **Encap dot1q 10** = This creates association of the ".1" sub-interface with the network which will have the third octet of "10". The "dot1q"

standard allows devices from different manufacturers to participate in vlans and Router-on-a-Stick. If the network only had Cisco Routers and Switches, another encapsulation protocol could be used called "ISL (Inter-Switch Link)".

19. Ip add 192.16.20.1 255.255.255.0 = Adds an IP address to the sub-interface.
20. No shut = This is an optional command which may not be necessary but it does not hurt.
21. End
22. Sh ip int brief = You will now see the sub-interface listed as if it is an actual physical interface.
23. Sh cdp neigh = Just to make sure that Router to ISP and 1st Floor Lab Switch can be reach each other. Now move to 1st Floor Lab Switch to configure it to communicate with the router.

- **1st Floor Lab Switch:**
  24. Conf t
  25. Int fa0/1
  26. **Switchport mode trunk** (This enables the interface to allow all vlan traffic to flow. (Special Note: The port encapsulation might also be changed if the interface is not compatible with "dot1q". The encapsulation can be changed to ISL with the command "Switchport encapsulation isl 10.")).

We must now create vlans on the switch. First, we will create the management VLAN on one of the switches:

- **On 1st Floor Lab Switch:**
  27. Config t
  28. (Config)# **vlan 10 (Gives the vlan a number reference)**
  29. (Config-vlan)# **name management (Optional to identify purpose).**
  30. (Config-vlan)# end
  31. **sh vlan** (Displays all vlans and associated interfaces. Now we will place one interface into VLAN 10)
     ☐ Config t
     ☐ (Config)# int fa0/5 = Connected to one of the PC's.
     ☐ (Config-if)# switchport access vlan 10
     ☐ (Config-if)# end
     ☐ # sh vlan (Shows interface fa0/5 in VLAN 10).
  32. **Sh run** (Readout under Fa0/5 displays that it is a member of VLAN 10.)

- **On any PC connected to 1st Floor Lab Switch** = Open a command prompt.
  33. **Type in the command "ipconfig /renew"** (The readout will display the ip address given from the DHCP server along with the Default gateway and Subnet mask. You can also check which IP's the DHCP Router have distributed by doing the following on Router "To ISP":
  34. **sh ip dhcp binding** = All devices which have been given an IP addresses along with their mac address.

Continue to create one of the communications subnets on the router.
- **On Router To ISP:**
  35. Conf t
  36. **Int fa0/0.2** (The ".2" creates a sub-interface which the terminal indicates is active.)
  37. **Encap dot1q 20** (This creates association of the ".2" subinterface with the network which will have the third octet of "20". The "dot1q" standard allows devices from different manufacturers to participate in vlans and Router-on-a-Stick. If the network only had Cisco Routers and Switches, another encapsulation protocol could be used called "ISL (Inter-Switch Link).)
  38. **Ip add 192.16.20.1 255.255.255.0** (Adds an IP address to the sub-interface.)
  39. No shut (This is an optional command which may not be necessary but it does not hurt.)
  40. End
  41. Sh ip int brief (You will now see the sub-interface listed as if it is an actual physical interface.)

To make sure that traffic can flow from the router to the switch, we will configure a DHCP scope for the 192.16.20.0 network by completing the following:
- **Logon to Router To ISP:**
  42. Conf t
  43. **Service DHCP** (This command enables/starts the service. Some routers will already have the service enabled by default.)
  44. **ip dhcp pool name 20Net** (Defines Configurations)
  45. **Network 192.16.20. 0 255.255.55.0** (Sets range)
  46. **Default-router 192.16.20.1** (Establishes Default Gateway)
  47. **Lease 0 0 5** (Time Device can keep IP settings)
  48. End <enter>

49. Sh run (You should now see the settings for DHCP towards the top of the readout.)

Although DHCP is operating, PC's will not get IP information because the vlans have not been created. We must now create vlans on the switch.

- **Log onto 1st Floor Lab Switch:**
  50. #Config t
  51. **(Config)# vlan 20** (Creates Vlan)
  52. **(Config-vlan)# name teachers** (Gives VLAN a name)
  53. (Config-vlan)# End <enter>
  54. **#sh vlan** (Displays all vlans and associated interfaces. Now we will place one interface into VLAN 20)
     - ☐ #Config t
     - ☐ (Config)# int fa0/6 (Connected to one of the PC's.)
     - ☐ **(Config-if)# switchport access vlan 20** (Associates port with VLAN)
     - ☐ (Config-if)# end <enter>
  55. **#sh vlan** (Shows interface fa0/6 in VLAN 20).
  56. Sh run (Readout under Fa0/6 displays that it is a member of VLAN 20.)
- **On PC2 = Open a command prompt.**
  57. Type in the command "ipconfig /renew".
  58. The readout will display the ip address given from the DHCP server along with the Default gateway and Subnet mask. You can also check which IP's the DHCP Router have distributed by doing the following:
- **On Router to ISP:**
  59. **sh ip dhcp binding** (Displays all devices which have been given an IP addresses along with their mac-address.)
  60. **Sh ip route** (Displays all networks the router can pass traffic between which includes both networks 192.16.10.0 and 192.16.20.0.)
- On PC1: Ping the default gateway for that network.
- On PC2: Ping the default gateway for that network.
- Ping between PC1 and PC2.

Router Voice Over IP:
Many companies and businesses experience rapid growth and changes within office buildings and locations. Oftentimes employees and staff members relocate to different offices which may not be in the same building or even located in different cities such as in the case of national companies that have

multiple branch offices. Many times the process of installing new telephone cabling and assigning new telephone numbers to those employees becomes the job of a network administrator or someone inside the technology department. Many organizations now utilize what is defined as "converged-networks" which simply means the network infrastructure within a building or company includes more than computer and printer connections. In many organizations the services which support telephones, video cameras, ID-security readers, audio-speaker systems and even office copiers are all part of the network supported by routers, switches and hubs. Working with Cisco devices it is essential that the technician have an understanding related to establishing a network supporting many of the above described services. One of the services would be configuring and maintaining telephone systems within an organization utilizing a technology defined as "Voice over IP (VoIP)". The following scenario gives an overview of establishing telephone communications utilizing Cisco routers, Cisco switches and VoIP telephone systems.

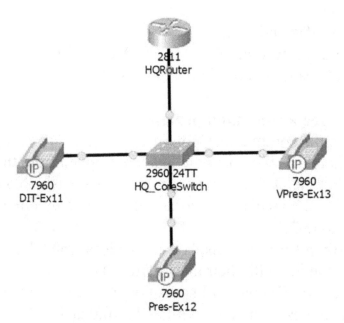

It is understood this equipment would be quite expensive for an individual to practice so it is recommended that various simulation software be utilized to configure a network as illustrated in the following instructions.

- **Equipment to be used:**
  - o Cisco VoIP Capable Router (1)
  - o Cisco Switch (1)
  - o VoIP Phones (At least 3)
  - o Associated cables for connections.

- **Router Configurations:** It is necessary to configure this router to distribute IP addresses across multiple network to support VoIP Services. Because DHCP and Router-On-A-Stick was previously covered in this text the commands will appear below but will not be explained in detail.

  - **Router-On-A-Stick Setup:**
    - ❖ Router(config)#int fa0/0
    - ❖ Router(config-if)#no shut
    - ❖ Router(config)#exit
    - ❖ Router(config)#int fa0/0.10
    - ❖ Router(config-if-subif)encap dot1q 10
    - ❖ Router(config-if-subif)#ip add 172.16.10.1 255.255.255.0
    - ❖ Router(config-if-subif)#exit
    - ❖ Router(config)#int fa0/0.20
    - ❖ Router(config-if-subif)encap dot1q 20
    - ❖ Router(config-if-subif)#ip add 172.16.20.1 255.255.255.0
    - ❖ Router(config-if-subif)#exit
    - ❖ Router(config)#int fa0/0.30
    - ❖ Router(config-if-subif)encap dot1q 30
    - ❖ Router(config-if-subif)#ip add 172.16.30.1 255.255.255.0
    - ❖ Router(config-if-subif)#exit

  - **Router DHCP Setup:**
    1. Router(config)#ip dhcp pool 10man
    2. Router(dhcp-config)#network 172.16.10.0 255.255.255.0
    3. Router(dhcp-config)#default-router 172.16.10.1
    4. Router(dhcp-config)#exit
    5. Router(config)#ip dhcp pool 20Net
    6. Router(dhcp-config)#network 172.16.20.0 255.255.255.0
    7. Router(dhcp-config)#default-router 172.16.20.1
    8. Router(dhcp-config)#exit
    9. Router(config)#ip dhcp pool 30voice
    10. Router(dhcp-config)#network 172.16.30.0 255.255.255.0
    11. Router(dhcp-config)#default-router 172.16.30.1
    12. Router(dhcp-config)#option 150 ip 172.16.30.1
    13. Router(dhcp-config)#exit

  - **Call Manager Express Setup:** "Call Manager Express" is a service included in the operating systems of some Cisco routers. It allows the router to support various telephony functions such as telephone numbers, multiple lines per telephone as well as voicemail and video-call functions. To configure the service is a multi-stage process which requires activating the service, configuring all of the telephone numbers, specifying the call manager as well as the total number of telephones to be supported. The following tasks must be performed:

1. Router(config)#telephony-service (Activates service)
2. Router(config-telephony)#max-dn 5 (Defines amount of telephone numbers available)
3. Router(config-telephony)#max-ephones 5 (Defines amount of phones)
4. Router(config-telephony)#ip source-address 172.16.30.1 port 2000 (Identifies Call Manager device and port for communications)
5. Router(config-telephony)#auto assign 1 to 5 (Allows phone numbers to be automatically set up on attached phones)

o **Associate Extensions (Numbers) with Phones:**
1. Router(config-ephone-dn)#ephone-dn 1 (Connect to first phone)
2. Router(config-ephone-dn)#number 11 (Assign extension "11")
3. Router(config-ephone-dn)#ephone-dn 2 (Connect to second phone)
4. Router(config-ephone-dn)#number 12 (Assign extension "12")
5. Router(config-ephone-dn)#ephone-dn 3 (Connect to third phone)
6. Router(config-ephone-dn)#number 13 (Assign extension "13")
7. Router(config-ephone-dn)#exit
8. Router(config)#exit

o **Switch VLAN Configuration (#18 is the most important!):**
1. Switch(config)#int fa0/1
2. Switch(config-if)#Switchport mode trunk
3. Switch(config-if)#exit
4. Switch(config)#vlan 10
5. Switch(config-vlan)#name man
6. Switch(config-vlan)#exit
7. Switch(config)#vlan 20
8. Switch(config-vlan)#name staff
9. Switch(config-vlan)#exit
10. Switch(config)#vlan 30
11. Switch(config-vlan)#name voice
12. Switch(config-vlan)#exit
13. Switch(config)#int range fa0/5 - 10

14. Switch(config-if-range)#switchport vlan 20
15. Switch(config-if-range)#exit
16. Switch(config)#int range fa0/11 - 20
17. Switch(config-if-range)#switchport mode access
18. Switch(config-if-range)#switchport voice vlan 30 (Allows switch to participate in VoIP operations)
19. Switch(config-if-range)#exit

At this time the telephone extension numbers should begin to appear on the view screens of the telephones. Some models of VoIP phones will also display the IP address the device has been assigned. After confirming all configurations your telephone system is now active and ready to be used.

Chapter 18
Network Security
Concepts and Methods

Network Security Concepts and Methods:

Cisco devices and operating systems have a number of features related to securing access and paths into networks. Some methods will totally mask the existence of a device while allowing connections to services such as Web or E-Mail. Other methods will allow only specific network devices to access specific devices. In addition, some features provide warnings as well as hide the identity of authorized users. Many of the methods have different utilizations of passwords, IP addresses, usernames, software and a multitude of others. The following sections will give an overview of some well-known methods.

Network Device Identification Configuration:

Oftentimes, the hostname of network devices are extremely unique and ambiguous. It is possible for a network administrator to connect remotely to a network device and make changes only to discover that it was not the correct device. In addition, in order to prosecute persons who access network devices without permission, there must be some outward and blatant indication of the device's private ownership and that unauthorized access will be charged legally. In order to compensate for the warning and identification issues, there are some methods to embed identity and legal message which displays upon user access. These messages will display in a terminal emulator window and are often called "Banners". The following exercises require PC1 and Switch1 from the previous exercises to create two different banners.

- **MOTD (Message of the Day)** = This will appear anytime an emulator connects to a network device for command line functions. The following is the process for creating a MOTD banner.
    1. Config t
    2. **Banner motd x** (The "x" is the ENDING CHARACTER of the message).
    3. Type the message "Access is prohibited"
    4. Now type the letter "x" (This will end the message).
    5. End
    6. sh run
    7. The message of the day displays towards the bottom of the readout.
    8. Exit
    9. Press the "enter" key and the message of the day will appear.
- **Login Banner** = This will appear anytime an emulator connects to a network device which requires a password login such as "enable" or "telnet".

1. Config t
2. **Banner login x** (The "x" is the ENDING CHARACTER of the message).
3. Type the message "You are accessing this device remotely. Please disconnect if unauthorized".
4. Now type the letter "x" (This will end the message).
5. End
6. Sh run
7. The message of the day displays towards the bottom of the readout.
8. Exit
9. Go to PC1 and activate the terminal emulator for Telnet.
10. Telnet to 172.16.10.2
11. Both the MOTD and the LOGIN banner will now appear.

Password Security Configuration and Exercise:

It can be noticed that all passwords are all listed in the "Show run" readouts which is a security concern. There are a number of methods to protect the access to the passwords. The following are some of the options:

- **Enable "Secret" Password** = When used, this will "scramble and replace" the characters displayed when reading the enable password on a switch or router. The technician will have to remember what the password is without a written display. If the password is every forgotten, some type of "password recovery" will have to be utilized to access and make changes to the network device. The following is the process for configuring an enable secret password:
    1. Config t
    2. **Enable Secret secret1** (The first two words are the commands. The last word "secret1" will actually become the password.)
    3. End <enter>
    4. Sh run (Now notice that there is "enable secret 5" line followed with characters similar to "1mERr$.mZUxVw4tp.fz.HSTl9q3/". This simply lets the technician know that there is a password but it is scrambled or what is referred to as "encrypted". (Note: If a switch or router has both a normal and "secret" enable password, only the "secret" password will be used. The cleartext enable password will display but will not operate).)

- **Securing all Passwords** = The previous exercise illustrates the process for making the "enable" password more secure, there are still other password which are in cleartext (Can be easily read). Passwords other than the secret password can be encrypted by utilizing a feature called "Password Encryption". The following will scramble all passwords which exist on the switch or router:
  1. Config t
  2. **Service password-encryption**
  3. End <enter>
  4. sh run (Now all passwords will display in an "encrypted" format.)

Switch Port Security:

On some networks it is important that specific devices stay exactly where they are connected. This can be the situation in which particular network sections require heightened security or if particular ports participate in services such as VoIP, video cameras or remote access. Since networks have hundreds of ports available in various buildings and locations it is impossible for a network administrator to assure that all devices are connected appropriately or not disconnected without approval. An example is the illustration below. In this topology notice there are telephones connected to particular ports in the switch. Often times when VoIP phones or other devices are connected to switches the ports must be configured specifically for those communications. In addition there may be other services directly associated with the MAC address of the port on the switch and the MAC address of the phone. In this scenario, it is essential that the telephone is not disconnected from that port as well as not be connected to any port.

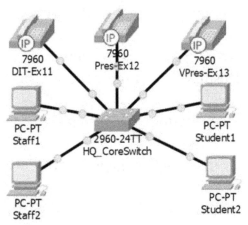

To control situation such as this there is an option on switches called "Port Security" which ensure specific devices are not disconnected as well as messages to be sent to a network administrators to announce changed connections. After configuring Port Security if a device other than what was originally established for the port is connected one of the following could be the result:

- **Protect** = Port stays on but discards communications from new device.
- **Restrict** = Port stays on, discards communications from new device and sends a SNMP message to the network administrator.
- **Shutdown (Default)** = Shutdowns port and sends a SNMP message to the network administrator (Note: If a port is shut down due to this setting the only way to activate the port is to either unplug the offending device or perform a "shutdown" followed by a "no shut" on the interface.

The following is an example of how to configure Port Security:

- **Equipment to be used (Just Essentials):**
  o At least 1 Cisco switch.
  o At least 1 VoIP Phone (Must have been active earlier).
  o Associated cables for connections.

- **Switch Configurations:**
  1. (Config)# int fa0/10 (Identifies which port to be used)
  2. (Config-if)# switchport mode access (Gives MAC address priority to port configurations)
  3. (Config-if)# switchport port-security (Activates security)
  4. (Config-if)# switchport port-security mac-address AAAA.BBBB.AAAA (Defines MAC of device allowed to connect to port)
  5. (Config-if)# switchport port-security violation {shutdown or restrict or protect} (Result of communications with unknown device).

After configuring port security it is possible to view the settings by using the following commands:
- **sh port-security address** = Displays all MACs and ports involved in port security.
- **sh port-security** = Displays all port security settings on switch.
- **show port-security interface fa0/#** = Displays security settings on specific port.

At this point if the device with an unknown MAC address is connected to the specific port it will perform one of the violations as specified. Because of the difficulty of finding MAC addresses on devices it is possible to have the switch automatically accept a single MAC address to associate with a port or even a maximum number of different MAC's which could be accepted by the port. Some of the options for configurations would be as follows:

- **(Config-if)# switchport port-security mac-address 0BC0.0C95.72AF** = As illustrated before this would be for a specific MAC.
- **(Config-if)# switchport port-security mac-address sticky** = Learn the first MAC connected.
- **(Config-if)# switchport port-security maximum N** = Max number of MAC's to learn on the port as devices are connected.

Remote Access Configurations and Exercise:

Often times, technicians must access routers and switches remotely. In order to do this, there is a protocol which works over TCP/IP networks called "Telnet". This protocol is supported by many devices, uses a small amount of resources on network devices and can be run on extremely low-powered systems. The protocol is also pre-installed on almost every network operating system, although on many, it has to be activated. To configure a router or switch to use telnet, it must be activated using a console cable and local access. Afterwards, as long as the router or switch is connected to a network, if the device can respond to a "ping" it can also be connected to via telnet. In the following exercise, we will configure telnet using the following resources:

- Terminal Emulation Software (Teraterm in our exercises).
- Console cable (1)
- Straight cables (3)
- Windows PC = 172.16.10.10 255.255.255.0
- Router1 = Int Fa0/0 - 172.16.10.1 mask 255.255.255.0
- Switch1 = Int vlan 1 - 172.16.10.2 mask 255.255.255.0
- Telnet Configuration Process:
  1. Set IP address on PC as specified in instructions.
  2. Connect PC 1 to Switch using the console cable.
  3. Connect PC 1 network interface to Switch int fa0/3.
  4. Show Run = The readout will have an entry towards the bottom which begins "line vty 0 4 (Sometimes the last number will be greater than "4" which indicates additional lines of communication are available. Disregard if higher number appears. We will use this line).

```
line con 0
!
line vty 0 4
 login
line vty 5 15
 login
```

- Configure switch and assure IP settings:
    5. Conf t
    6. Int vlan 1
    7. Ip Add 172.16.10.2 255.255.255.0
    8. No shut
    9. Ping PC until receive five exclamation points (100% Successful).

Configure Telnet:

The ability to remotely manage network devices is extremely essential in the daily activities of network administrator. Depending on the geographic range of the network an individual can be responsible for routers and switches which exist in different cities but part of the same network. As illustrated earlier, Telnet is a very valuable tool which can be used to remotely configure routers and switches. The following is an example of how the service can be configured:

- **Configure Process:**
    1. Config T
    2. **Line vty 0 4** (You will notice that the prompt has changed indicating that you are using a "Line" (In essence, a "Communication Line").)
    3. **Login <enter>** (You may get a readout stating "Login Disabled until password is set. Disregard because you are now setting a password.)
    4. **Password telnet1** (This sets the telnet password to "telnet1". These passwords are case sensitive).)
    5. End
    6. Show run (After the "Line vty 0 4" statement, there now appears the password for telnet. Before telnet will operate, you will need to create an "enable" password as well.)
    7. Conf t
    8. Enable password enable1
    9. End
    10. Sh run (Towards the top of the readout, you will notice the enable password listed.)
    11. Disconnect the Console between the PC and the Switch.

- **Testing Telnet from a Terminal:**
  10. Go to the PC and ping the IP of the Switch until you get 100% responses (Five exclamation points).
  11. Activate command line telnet or use the terminal emulator.
  12. Input the IP address of the switch.
  13. The emulator displays "User Access Verification". This prompt is looking for the password setup for the "vty line 0 4" entry. Enter "telnet1".
  14. The login prompt is now displayed. This prompt is looking for the "enable" password. Enter "enable1" and press "enter".
  15. The name of the Switch now appears. At this point, all normal switch commands will work. Attempt the following to experiment:
     ➢ Change the Hostname of the Switch.
     ➢ Display all the interfaces on the switch.
     ➢ Display all the settings on the switch.
  16. To end the telnet session, type "exit".

- **Telnet between network devices** = It is possible to telnet from a switch to a router or visa-versa. The following is the process to configure the router for telnet and then connect to the router from the switch:
  1. Connect PC 1 to Router1 one using the console cable.
  2. Router1 Fa0/0 to Switch 1 Fa0/2 using a straight cable.
  3. Activate the terminal emulator to utilize the "console" connection.
  4. Show Run (The readout will have an entry towards the bottom which begins "line vty 0 4 (Sometimes the last number will be greater than "4" which indicates additional lines of communication are available. Disregard if higher number appears. We will use this line).)

- Configure Router1 and assure IP settings:
  1. Conf t
  2. Int Fa0/0
  3. Ip Add 172.16.10.1 255.255.255.0
  4. No shut
  5. Ping Switch1 until receive five exclamation points (100% Successful).
- **Configure Telnet:**
  1. Config T
  2. Line vty 0 4
  3. Login <enter>
  4. Password telnet1

5. End
6. Show run (After the "Line vty 0 4" statement, there now appears the password for telnet. Before telnet will operate, you will need to create an "enable" password as well.)
7. Conf t
8. Enable password enable1
9. End
10. Sh run (Towards the top of the readout, you will notice the enable password listed.)
11. Disconnect the Console between the PC and the router.
12. Reconnect the Console between the PC and the Switch.
13. Go to the emulator and ping the IP of the router until you get 100% responses (Five exclamation points).

- **Begin the telnet session:**
  1. Input "telnet 172.16.10.1" (Note: If you do not use the exact syntax, the emulator will begin display a number of questions. If it occurs,…I suggest typing "end" until back at the user prompt).
  2. The emulator displays "Trying 172.16.10.1…." followed by "User Access Verification". This prompt is looking for the password setup for the "vty line 0 4" entry. Enter "telnet1".
  3. The login prompt is now displayed. This prompt is looking for the "enable" password. Enter "enable1" and press "enter".
  4. The name of the Router now appears. At this point, all normal Router commands will work. Attempt the following to experiment:
     ➢ Change the Hostname of the Router.
     ➢ Display all the interfaces on the Router.
     ➢ Display all the settings on the Router.
  5. To end the telnet session, type "exit".

Secure Shell (SSH):

Telnet is a very valuable tool which can be used to remotely configure routers and switches. An inherent problem with Telnet however is the fact that it is a "clear text" protocol which essentially means that usernames, passwords and commands can be captured as the messages travel the network. This gives opportunity for cyber criminals to gain access to network devices compromising data or possibly disabling network devices. To combat this there are other command line options in which all communications are encrypted to provide a level of protection. One of the first levels of command line remote management protocols with protection is classified as "Secure Shell (SSH).

SSH allows remote management of network devices while providing end-to-end encryption of transmissions. The following is an example of how to configure a router or switch to use SSH.

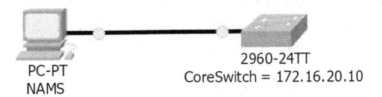

PC-PT
NAMS

2960-24TT
CoreSwitch = 172.16.20.10

- **Equipment to be used for SSH configuration:**
  - o At least 1 Cisco Switch (Same process is used on Routers).
  - o One Computer with telnet services installed and command line Access.
  - o Straight Category Cable.

- **SSH Configurations:**
  1. (config)#int vlan 1 (Activate virtual interface.)
  2. (config-if)#ip add 172.16.20.2 255.255.255.0 (Place IP address on interface.)
  3. (config-if)#no shut
  4. (config-if)#exit
  5. (config)#hostname CoreSwitch
  6. (config)#enable password epass (Telnet-related connections require an ENABLE password.)
  7. (config)#ip domain-name cool.com (SSH requires a domain name.)
  8. (config)#crypto key generate rsa (Higher levels of bits increase protection but also increases CPU Processing. Best practices is to select 1024 bits and type "yes" to either confirm or replace previous key as an following diagram:)

```
coreswitch(config)#crypto key generate rsa
The name for the keys will be: coreswitch.cool.com
Choose the size of the key modulus in the range of 360 to 2048 for your
  General Purpose Keys. Choosing a key modulus greater than 512 may take
  a few minutes.

How many bits in the modulus [512]: 1024
% Generating 1024 bit RSA keys, keys will be non-exportable...[OK]
```

  9. (config)#username dude1 password spass (Configures user account on switch.)
  10. (config)#ip ssh ver 2 (Assures Version 2 protection for communications.)
  11. (config)#line vty 0 4 (Range of channels may go as high as 15.)

12.(config-line)#transport input ssh (Engages SSH protocol.)

13.(config-line)#login local (Identifies which account will use SSH.)

14.(config-line)#end

At this point it will be required to open up a command line from a machine that can at least ping the switch. The command "ssh -l dude1 172.16.20.2 (This is an "L" and stands for "login" combined with the username on the switch followed by the switch IP address.)" would initiate the session. When the connection is established a prompt will appear first asking for the SSH password (spass) followed by a prompt for the enable password (epass).

```
Packet Tracer PC Command Line 1.0
C:\>ssh -l dude1 172.16.20.2
Open
Password:




CoreSwitch>en
Password:
CoreSwitch#
```

Once both passwords are accepted the switch will accept commands remotely while the transmissions have levels of protection.

Access Control List (ACL)

This method will allow the configuration of rules on a router which either permits or denies communications. ACLs create rules allowing traffic between sources and destinations. The source or destination can be a single host or a section of a network. Once an ACL is created, the router will compare all packets to the statements in the ACL and process it accordingly. ACL's appear in two types:

- **Standard ACL** = Establishes all rules of communication on the total IP address of sources or destinations.
- **Extended ACL** = Allows the creation of rules for specific protocols between source and destinations in order to delimit the use of accesses to websites, e-mail, ping requests, etc.
- **Named ACL's** = It is possible to use either numbers or names to create access lists. Both have advantages and disadvantages and it is normally just the desire of the network technician as to which is used.

- **ACL Elements:**
  - **Specific Interface** = After creation on a router, the ACL rule must be set to a specific interface and enabled. It is not automatically applied.
  - **Direction** = ACL statements can be applied to either the interface a packet will enter the router or the interface that the packet will exit the router.
  - **Implicit deny** = Once enabled on a router, only packets which match statements in the ACL will be processed. If a packet does not match a statement, it is rejected. This is called an "Implicit Deny".
  - **Wildcard Mask** = This is a way of modifying an inverse subnet mask which allows groups of computers to be affected by an ACL. (For the purpose of this book, wildcard masks will not be used).

Access Control List (ACL) Configuration Exercises:

The following exercises will utilize both numbered and named ACL's. These exercises require the completion of previous exercises for some instructions will not be specified because they should have been mastered from earlier labs. Required for this exercise will be as follows:
- Two Crossover cables.
- Terminal Emulator.
- Console Cable.
- Two PC's:
  - PC1 = IP add 172.16.20.10 mask 255.255.255.0 and a default gateway of 172.16.20.1
  - PC2 = IP add 172.16.30.10 mask 255.255.255.0 and a default gateway of 172.16.30.1.
- Router with two Fastethernet interfaces:
  - Fa0/0 with ip address 172.16.20.1 255.255.255.0
  - Fa0/1 with ip address 172.16.30.1 255.255.255.0

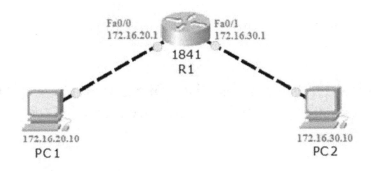

- **ACL exercise** = We will create an ACL which stops PC2 from communicating with PC1 by placing an entrance ACL on the FastEthernet connection:
  1. Connect the console between PC2 and R1.
  2. On PC 2 open the command prompt and ping PC1 until 3 to 5 positive replies occur.
  3. Turn on the Terminal Emulator and access R1 command line and perform the following commands:
  4. Config t
  5. **access-list 10 deny host 172.16.30.10** (This command identifies the ACL number and which host will be stopped.)
  6. Int fa0/1
  7. **ip access-group 10 in** (This command will apply the ACL to fa0/1 and process any packets which "enter" the router against the ACL statements.)
  8. End
  9. **sh access-lists** (Or "sh ip access-list" Displays all created lists and how many packets have been matched against the ACL.)
  10. Ping from PC2 to R1 (Notice that communications are blocked.)
  11. Ping from PC1 to R1 (You see that PC1 is also blocked due to the implicit deny. Let's now add a statement which would allow other packets thru the R1.)
  12. config t
  13. **access-list 10 permit any** (This will allow other traffic to pass thru the interface controlling for the "Implicit Deny".)
  14. Ping from PC2 to R1 (Notice that communications are still blocked.)
  15. Ping from PC1 to R1 (You see that PC1 can communicate with no difficulties.)
- **Creating a named access list for the same exercise:**
  1. **R1 (config)# ip access-list standard blockping** (Provides Name.)
  2. R1 (config-std-nacl)# deny host 172.16.30.10
  3. R1 (config-std-nacl)# permit any
  4. Int fa0/1
  5. **R1 (config-if)# ip access-group blockping in** (Associates ACL with interface.)
  6. End
  7. sh access-lists (Or "sh ip access-list". Displays all the new ACL's named list and how many packets have been matched against the ACL.)

Virtual Private Networks:

Many companies often use the Internet for various forms of commerce and communication. These transactions travel through a multitude of routers and other publicly owned devices. The routers and other Internet devices owned by various entities do not guarantee any security of the information traveling through them. There are many situations in which data is confidential and should be protected from being viewed, altered or forged. To combat the problem of data being compromised organization often utilize various types of software or other methods which afford a type of protection for communications simulating that the transmissions are occurring on a private network although actually transpiring on public lines of commerce. A well-known term to define the use of these protection options is often called "VPN (Virtual Private Network)".

GRE-VPN Exercise:

Cisco routers have a few options which support VPNS one of which is called "GRE (Generic Routing Encapsulation)". A simple description of GRE is a "tunnel" created inside a path used for communication between two remotely connected routers.

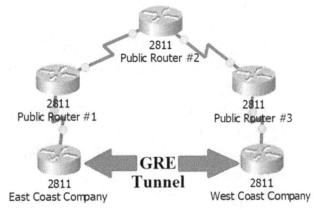

The routers are configured to "hide" the data being transmitted. The data travels through the multiple devices but cannot be read by any of them (Unless compromised by a highly proficient "Hacker"). In addition, the routers included in the VPN are often configured to only accept communications from other routers configured for the GRE-VPN. The following is an example of configuring a GRE-VPN for company with branch offices separated by multiple public routers.

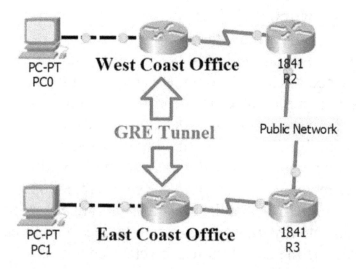

The following is an example of configuring a GRE VPN Tunnel for company with branch offices separated by multiple public routers.

- **Equipment to be used:**
  - o At least four Cisco routers and associated cables.

- **Router Configurations:**
  - ➤ **West Coast Router (WCR):**
    1. WCR(config)#inter tunnel 0 (Creates GRE session)
    2. WCR(config-if)#ip add 10.10.10.1 255.0.0.0
    3. WCR(config)#no shut
    4. WCR(config-if)#tunnel source s0/0/0 (Interface on this router pointing to destination network)
    5. WCR(config-if)#tunnel destination 172.16.40.2 (IP on receiving router interface)
    6. WCR(config)#ip route 172.16.50.0 255.255.255.0 10.10.10.2 (Setting for GRE Route)

  - ➤ **East Coast Router (ECR):**
    1. ECR(config)#interface tunnel 0
    2. ECR(config-if)#ip add 10.10.10.2 255.0.0.0
    3. ECR(config)#no shut
    4. ECR(config-if)#tunnel source s0/0/1
    5. ECR(config-if)#tunnel destination 172.16.20.1
    6. ECR(config)#ip route 172.16.10.0 255.255.255.0 10.10.10.1

After the tunnel has been configured on the devices the following commands can be used to display their status and condition:

- show ip interface tunnel
- show ip tunnel traffic
- show interface tunnel
- show statistics tunnel

IPSec-VPN Exercise:

Much communications between large organizations often traverse public networks. International companies which have offices in different countries would be an example of communications utilizing routers and network devices owned by organizations other than themselves. Due to communications and commerce traveling through unsecured networks there is always the potential that information can be compromised in some form. In network technology, there are multiple ways in which data communications can be protected from compromise while traveling public network infrastructures. One methodology used on Cisco devices is in the form of encrypting traffic as it travels through public network devices. The frames or packets travel through public devices is in a format that is illegible to those devices. The data is configured in a format designed to be viewed and understood by the sending and receiving points. A comparison of encrypted communications would be similar to a person putting a gift inside of a box before they send it through the mail. The mailperson would pick up the box but has no idea of what is actually inside of the container. The box would pass through many locations and mailpersons who also have no idea of the boxes' contents. Eventually the box arrives at its destination and the receiving person opens the box to reveal its contents. This is similar to the process of encapsulation which is when messages are inside of a larger message customized for communications between the sender and destination. Not only is the data provided a level of protection but there is also included "Authentication" methods to confirm the identity of the sender as well as ensuring that the data within the transmission has not been compromised.

In order to configure various options related to encapsulation and authentication requires the utilization of various protocols, software and methods. Some elements related to encapsulation would be the following:

- **Crypto Map** = Configured on a network device which identifies data which should be secured and the devices which will participate in the communications often defined as "Peers".

- **Internet Security Association and Key Management Protocol (ISAKMP)** = Supports security key creation and authentication between devices participating in protected communications.
- **Internet Protocol Security (IPSEC)** = Allows encryption of data at the IP level.
- **Security-Association** = A definition of how end points will communicate over public environments utilizing various protection schemes such as encryption, VPN's and encapsulation.
- **Advanced Encryption Standard (AES)** = Method of protecting data based upon a groupings of bits traditionally in blocks of 128, 192 or 256 bits.
- **Authentication** = Process of validating the identity of sender and receivers prior to accepting transmitted data or communications.
- **Pre-Shared Key** = String of code possessed by participating devices used to validate identities for data transfer or communication.
- **Diffie-Hellman Groups** = Identifiers for levels of key security. The higher the "Group #" the more bits included in a security block supporting higher potential of protection (i.e., Group 1 = 768 bits, Group 5 = 1536 bits, Group 15 = 3072 bits, etc.).
- **Transform-Set** = Combined rules of configurations which supported data encryption and authentication within VPNs and other encapsulated means of communications.
- **Perfect Forward Secrecy (PFS)** = Encryption process which assures the generation of unique keys used to secure data transmissions not related to any previously used keys.

The diagram below illustrates a topology related to an IPSec-VPN tunnel connecting a network of 200.200.200.0 to another network of 100.100.100.0 using public routers on the Internet. Following the graphic there is a walk-thru of how to configure routers to support authenticated and encrypted communications.

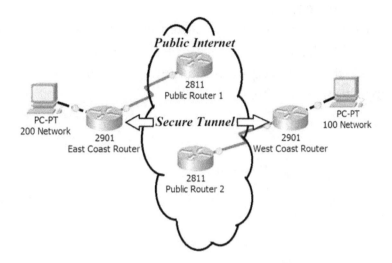

- **Equipment to be used for IPSec-VPN configuration:**
  - At least 2 Cisco Routers (Exercise will include four Routers).
  - At least two Computers.
  - Required connection cables (May be Category or Serial).
  - Special Notes before configuration:
    - ➤ Establish a routing protocol between routers to support pinging all devices (Using RIP might be the easiest for testing purposes).
    - ➤ Have Hostnames on Routers.
    - ➤ Assure endpoint routers have a security package license available (Use "sh ver" to confirm and once active it will display as "securityk9").
    - ➤ Any name can be used for the pre-shared key and name of security set. We will use "200to100" for both.
    - ➤ The ACL number "110" is an example, not a requirement. Any extended ACL number would work.

- **East Coast Router (EC_Router) Configurations:**
  1. EC_Router>enable
  2. EC_Router#sh ver (Displays the active licenses on the router, notice there is no active security modules).

```
Technology Package License Information for Module:'c2900'

---------------------------------------------------------------
Technology    Technology-package          Technology-package
              Current      Type           Next reboot
---------------------------------------------------------------
ipbase        ipbasek9     Permanent      ipbasek9
security      disable      None           None
uc            disable      None           None
data          disable      None           None

Configuration register is 0x2102
```

3. EC_Router#config t
4. EC_Router (config)# license boot module c2900 technology-package securityk9 (Loads the security module to become active after the next reboot. It will be required to enter "yes", save the configurations and then reboot the router).

```
Activation  of the  software command line interface will be evidence of
your acceptance of this agreement.

ACCEPT? [yes/no]: yes  <===
% use 'write' command to make license boot config take effect on next boot
%LICENSE-6-EULA_ACCEPTED: EULA for feature securityk9 1.0 has been accepted. UDI=CISCO2901/
K9:FTX15240ZPA; StoreIndex=0:Evaluation License Storage

EastCoastRouter(config)#: %IOS_LICENSE_IMAGE_APPLICATION-6-LICENSE_LEVEL: Module name = C2900 Next
reboot level = securityk9 and License = securityk9

EastCoastRouter(config)#|
```

5. EC_Router (config)# Exit
6. EC_Router#copy run start (Saving new configurations.)
7. EC_Router#reload (Confirm save and "enter" to reload.)
8. EC_Router>enable
9. EC_Router # sh ver (Displays "securityk9" license is now active.)

```
Technology Package License Information for Module:'c2900'

-----------------------------------------------------------------
Technology    Technology-package          Technology-package
              Current       Type          Next reboot
-----------------------------------------------------------------
ipbase        ipbasek9      Permanent     ipbasek9
security      securityk9    Evaluation    securityk9  <===
uc            disable       None          None
data          disable       None          None

Configuration register is 0x2102
```

10. EC_Router#config t
11. EC_Router (config)# crypto isakmp policy 30 (Creating policy with "30" as identifier).
12. EC_Router (config-isakmp)# encryption aes 256 (Bits to use.)
13. EC_Router (config-isakmp)# authentication pre-share (Key to be used.)
14. EC_Router (config-isakmp)# group 5 (Diffie-Hellman, 1536 Bits)
15. EC_Router (config-isakmp)# exit

16. EC_Router (config)# crypto isakmp key 200to100 address 172.16.30.2 (Naming key and participating West Coast Router address.)
17. EC_Router (config)# access-list 110 permit ip 200.200.200.0 0.0.0.255 100.100.100.0 0.0.0.255 (ACL map for source and destination.)
18. EC_Router (config)# crypto ipsec transform-set 200to100 esp-aes 256 esp-sha-hmac (Creating key, authentication and encapsulation set.)
19. EC_Router (config)# crypto map 200to100 110 ipsec-isakmp (Linking ACL to map.)
20. EC_Router (config)# set transform-set 200to100 (Linking set to map. Display warning that settings are not complete until participating router is configured and active.)

```
EastCoastRouter(config)#crypto map 200to100 110 ipsec-isakmp
% NOTE: This new crypto map will remain disabled until a peer
        and a valid access list have been configured.
EastCoastRouter(config-crypto-map)#|
```

21. EC_Router (config-crypto-map)# set peer 172.16.30.2 (Identifies West Coast Router as partner.)
22. EC_Router (config-crypto-map)# set pfs group5 (Ensures unique key.)
23. EC_Router (config-crypto-map)# set security-association lifetime seconds 86400 (How long rules will be valid.)
24. EC_Router (config-crypto-map)# match address 110 (Links association to ACL.)
25. EC_Router (config-crypto-map)# exit
26. EC_Router (config)# int s0/2/0 (Interface to be used on this Router.)
27. EC_Router (config-if)# crypto map 200to100 (Connects interface to rule set. A message will display showing configurations are engaged. Ignore the "off" statement.)

```
EastCoastRouter(config)#int s0/2/0
EastCoastRouter(config-if)#crypto map 200to100
*Jan  3 07:16:26.785: %CRYPTO-6-ISAKMP_ON_OFF: ISAKMP is ON
```

28. EC_Router (config-if)#end

At this point you should use the "sh crypto ipsec sa" command to display the active configurations. Pay close attention to the section related to "encaps" and "decaps" which displays any communications. At present, there should be done but after configurations are completed on the peer router they will appear after successful communications between the 200 network and the 100 network. To continue the IPSec-VPN tunnel, move onto the peer router and perform the configurations below:

- **West Coast Router (WC_Router) Configurations:**
    1. WC_Router>enable
    2. WC_Router# sh ver
    3. WC_Router#config t
    4. WC_Router (config)# license boot module c2900 technology-package securityk9
    5. WC_Router (config)# Exit
    6. WC_Router#copy run start
    7. WC_Router#reload
    8. WC_Router>enable
    9. WC_Router # sh ver (Displays "securityk9" license is now active.)
    10. WC_Router#config t
    11. WC_Router (config)# crypto isakmp policy 30
    12. WC_Router (config-isakmp)# encryption aes 256
    13. WC_Router (config-isakmp)# authentication pre-share
    14. WC_Router (config-isakmp)# group 5
    15. WC_Router (config-isakmp)# exit
    16. WC_Router (config)# crypto isakmp key 200to100 address 172.16.10.1 (This links the East Coast Router.)
    17. WC_Router (config)# access-list 110 permit ip 100.100.100.0 0.0.0.255 200.200.200.0 0.0.0.255 (This is the REVERSE of the ACL on East Coast Router.)
    18. WC_Router (config)# crypto ipsec transform-set 200to100 esp-aes 256 esp-sha-hmac
    19. WC_Router (config)# crypto map 200to100 110 ipsec-isakmp
    20. WC_Router (config)# set transform-set 200to100
    21. WC_Router (config-crypto-map)# set peer 172.16.10.1 (Identifies East Coast Router as partner.)
    22. WC_Router (config-crypto-map)# set pfs group5
    23. WC_Router (config-crypto-map)# set security-association lifetime seconds 86400
    24. WC_Router (config-crypto-map)# match address 110
    25. WC_Router (config-crypto-map)# exit
    26. WC_Router (config)# int s0/2/1
    27. WC_Router (config-if)# crypto map 200to100
    28. WC_Router (config-if)#end

At this stage, initiate pings between the computers in the different networks. Encapsulation processes will fail for the first few attempts followed by successful communications. After successful pings, use the "sh crypto ipsec sa" command on either router and notice there are now entries for "encaps" and "decaps" as well as other items in the display.

```
WestCoastRouter#sh crypto ipsec sa

interface: Serial0/2/1
    Crypto map tag: 200to100, local addr 172.16.30.2

  protected vrf: (none)
  local  ident (addr/mask/prot/port): (100.100.100.0/255.255.255.0/0/0)
  remote ident (addr/mask/prot/port): (200.200.200.0/255.255.255.0/0/0)
  current_peer 172.16.10.1 port 500
    PERMIT, flags={origin is acl,}
   #pkts encaps: 19, #pkts encrypt: 19, #pkts digest: 0
   #pkts decaps: 18, #pkts decrypt: 18, #pkts verify: 0
   #pkts compressed: 0, #pkts decompressed: 0
   #pkts not compressed: 0, #pkts comp. failed: 0
   #pkts not decompressed: 0, #pkts decompress failed: 0
   #send errors 1, #recv errors 0

    local crypto endpt.: 172.16.30.2, remote crypto endpt.:172.16.10.1
    path mtu 1500, ip mtu 1500, ip mtu idb Serial0/2/1
    current outbound spi: 0x79126AA2(2031250082)

    inbound esp sas:
     spi: 0x7B115BAA(2064735146)
       transform: esp-aes 256 esp-sha-hmac ,
       in use settings ={Tunnel, }
       conn id: 2002, flow_id: FPGA:1, crypto map: 200to100
       sa timing: remaining key lifetime (k/sec): (4525504/86319)
       IV size: 16 bytes
       replay detection support: N
       Status: ACTIVE
```

Additional helping commands would include the following:
- **sh crypto isakmp policy** = Displays all policies.
- **sh crypto map** = Displays all set rules and peers.
- **sh crypto ?** = Displays additional related options.

IP Translation Methods:

Many companies are connected to the internet through various methods. Often times, internal company servers are required to be accessible from outside of the actual network. Each server requires an IP address which can be contacted outside of the company or business (Often called a "Public" address). Inside the network, however, the same servers are connected to by using an internal IP address (Often called a "Private" address). It is possible to utilize a public IP address on all internal servers but the process is costly and very unsecure. If a server is directly connected to the internet, it would lose a lot of its security features and layers of protection offered by a DMZ (Demilitarized Zone). In order to allow outside access to internal servers, there are methods of connecting, or actually converting outside public connections to internal private connections. Some of the methods and their elements are illustrated in the following paragraphs and labs.

- **Network Address Translation (NAT)** allows a connection between an address inside of a LAN or Private network using an address which is outside of the private network such as the internet. In the diagram below, a user on the internet is connecting to the video server by using one address on the public interface on the router. The router has a range of IP addresses available on the internet and each IP is directly connected to a different internal company server. Since each IP is dedicated to a different server, this may increase the cost of the router or make the management of the router more complicated. Notice that 165.95.58.92 is directly related to 10.10.10.30:

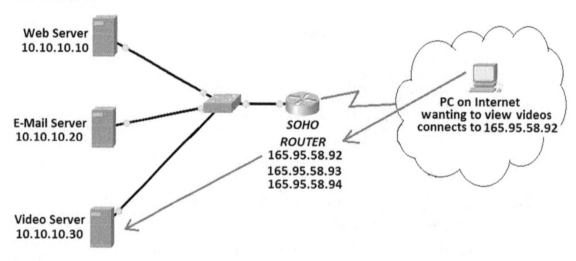

- **Port Address Translation (PAT)** allows the connection of an internal network (LAN or Private) address to be accessed via a single outside public address which is linked to a specific port of communication (In reference to the 65,535 available ports such as port 80, 23, 21, etc. Also, on SOHO networks (Small Office-Home Office) this process is often referred to as "Port Forwarding"). In the scenario below, a user on the internet desires to access a server inside of a company which provides access to videos. The company only makes available a single IP address but links each server to the IP address using a different port number. In order to connect to the Video Server, the user opens a browser and in the address bar types in "HTTPS://165.95.58.92:7001" which leads to the public interface on the router which passes the request to the server with the IP address of 10.10.10.30 which is linked to port "7001".

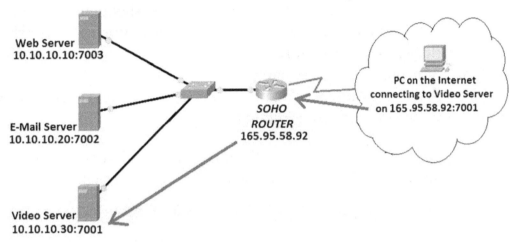

NAT Configuration Exercise:

The following are instruction for a lab to configure NAT. Using the topology below, we will configure NAT on the "DMZ Router" to allow the computers outside of the network (On the "ISP-Side") to access the Web Server inside the network ("DMZ-Side")".

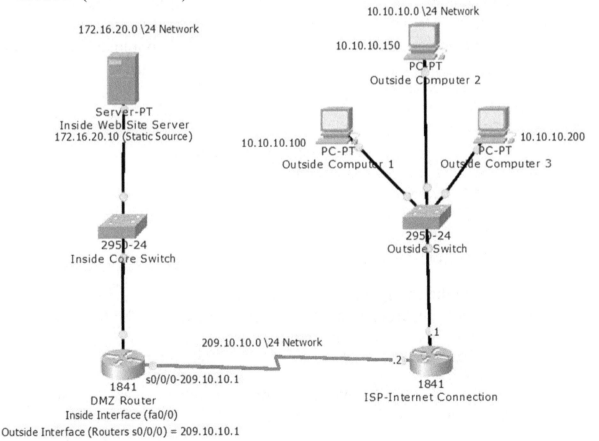

In order to start the process, we will need to consider and configure the following NAT Elements:

- **Create Translation** = Process the router should use to direct public/outside network IP traffic to private/internal network devices.
- **Select inside interface** = Router interface connected to LAN (Inside of network/Private Facing).
- **Select outside interface** = Router interface connected to WAN (Outside of network/Public Facing).

The target server hosts a website with an internal IP address of "172.16.20.10". Accessing the website using the "outside client" the following occurs:

TeachTechnologies.Net
Company Website Server

It is desired that clients outside of the private network (Such as those outside of a company on the Internet) use a public advertised IP address of "209.10.10.1". The following commands are utilized on "DMZ_Router" to implement NAT in the offered environment:

- DMZ_Router> en
- DMZ_Router# conf t
- DMZ_Router(config)# ip nat inside source static 172.16.20.10 209.10.10.1 (This is all one line).
- DMZ_Router(config)# int fa0/0
- DMZ_Router(config-if)# ip nat inside
- DMZ_Router (config)# int s0/0/0
- DMZ_Router(config-if)# ip nat outside

After completing the configurations, it is best to confirm your settings prior to attempting connections from an outside system. The first method you could use is the "Show Run" command as in the following:

- DMZ_Router# Show run
  - This will display the interfaces which are either "inside" or "outside" as well as the NAT translation statement.

interface FastEthernet0/0
ip address 172.16.20.1 255.255.255.0
ip nat inside

o And:
ip nat inside source static 172.16.20.10 209.10.10.1

Another option to confirm NAT configurations is via the use of the
"Sh ip nat translations" command:

- DMZ_Router# Sh ip nat translations
  DMZ_Router#sh ip nat trans
  Pro Inside global   Inside local   Outside local   Outside global
  --- 209.10.10.1   172.16.20.10   ---   ---

  o The first time this command is run it will display the configurations only.
    After traffic has passed thru the router from the interface to the target
    device (In this case the web server) it will report additional information.

After confirming the settings, we access the webserver via the outside client
10.10.10.150 by using the routers reported IP address off HTTPS://209.10.10.1
and the website appears:

TeachTechnologies.Net
Company Website Server

After successful communications occur through NAT, additional information is
displayed after using the "sh ip nat translations" as in the following:

DMZ_Router#sh ip nat trans
Pro Inside global   Inside local   Outside local   Outside global
--- 209.10.10.1   172.16.20.10   ---   ---
tcp 209.10.10.1:80   172.16.20.10:80   10.10.10.150:1025 10.10.10.150:1025

The report created by the "show ip nat translations" command will display IP related information about all systems participating in a NAT communication as in the following:

- **Inside Global** = IP address of the inside network target device as viewed from the Internet (Public Network).
- **Inside Local** = IP address of the inside network target device as viewed from the inside of the network (Private Network).
- **Outside Local** = The reported IP address of the device outside of the private network (Such as the internet) displayed inside of the private network.
- **Outside Global** = The reported public IP address of the client outside of the private network displayed on the public network (The Internet).

It is also possible to see more detailed reports concerning the number of systems which are utilizing the NAT translation via the following **"sh ip nat statistics"** command as in the following:

```
DMZ_Router#sh ip nat statistics
Total translations: 2 (1 static, 1 dynamic, 1 extended)
Outside Interfaces: Serial0/0/0
Inside Interfaces: FastEthernet0/0
Hits: 7  Misses: 67
Expired translations: 0
Dynamic mappings:
DMZ_Router#
```

The entries in the NAT log can become very large and viewing can be difficult because of the increasing numbers of entries. In the event that it is necessary to check new settings, it is possible to remove log transactions via using the "clear ip nat translations" command. NAT will still function, but all the previous connection attempts will be removed from the display.

DNS and Hostname Resolution:

When using command line on routers, occasionally, a typo will occur and the result is the router attempting to locate a network device or host which has a name identical to the incorrect entry. This occurs because the router is attempting to use the "Domain Name System (DNS)" or any available "Host

Table". The router will continue to attempt to locate the incorrect host until it is successful or the requests times out as in the following example:

```
DMZ_Router#
DMZ_Router#vids
Translating "vids"...domain server (255.255.255.255)
% Unknown command or computer name, or unable to find computer address
```

During the time the router is attempting the DNS search, it is impossible to issue commands to the router using the same terminal connection. In order to avoid this problem, there are three options:

- **Option #1** = Configure the router not to attempt DNS searches with the **"no ip domain-lookup"** command as in the following:

  o DMZ_Router (Config)# no ip domain-lookup.
  o DMZ_Router (Config)# end

Now the router will no longer attempt to locate devices using hostnames. The router will simply respond that the device cannot be located. Refer to the following graphic:

```
DMZ_Router(config)#no ip domain-lookup
DMZ_Router(config)#exit
DMZ_Router#
%SYS-5-CONFIG_I: Configured from console by console

DMZ_Router#vids
Translating "vids"
% Unknown command or computer name, or unable to find computer address
```

- **Option #2 = Configure the router to use a DNS server** which performs resolutions for the entire network. Using this method, the router is configured to send all host requests to a server or router which can perform DNS resolution. The following commands would be required:

  o DMZ_Router (Config)#ip domain-lookup (This command enables DNS resolution in case it was disabled)
  o DMZ_Router (Config)#**ip name server 8.8.8.8** (IP address of a DNS provider)
  o DMZ_Router (Config)#end

Now it would be possible to ping or telnet into a device by using the DNS name (And sometimes a simple hostname).

- **Option #3 = Create a host table on the router** in which DNS names will be used for connections. It is possible for a router to host its own host table. In this way, the routers can locate network devices using hostnames instead of addresses. Using a hostname is often helpful when using telnet as a method to control or access a network device. In this example, it is desired to locate "DMZ Router" from the "ISP Router" by using the name "DMZ".

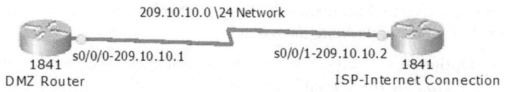

209.10.10.0 \24 Network

1841   s0/0/0-209.10.10.1   s0/0/1-209.10.10.2   1841
DMZ Router   ISP-Internet Connection

The DMZ Router has an ip address of "209.10.10.1". Normally, in order to access the DMZ Router, a computer would have to use the IP address for a successful connection as in the following graphic:

```
ISP#telnet 209.10.10.1
Trying 209.10.10.1 ...Open
User Access Verification

Password:
DMZ_Router>en
Password:
DMZ_Router#
```

Next, we attempt the same action using the hostname without success:
```
ISP>en
ISP#telnet dmz
Translating "dmz"...domain server (255.255.255.255)
% Unknown command or computer name, or unable to find computer address
```

The following would be the process to configure a "Host Record" for the DMZ Router so the ISP Router can use a hostname (Note, this would only allow the ISP Router to locate the host. Any other routers requiring the use of hostnames would have to have the entry added to that routers host table.). The process for creating a host table on ISP Router is as follows:

- ISP_Router# Config t
- ISP_Router#(config)# **ip host dmz 209.10.10.1**
- ISP_Router#(config)# end

To confirm the settings, perform the "show hosts" command:

```
ISP>en
ISP#sh hosts
Default Domain is not set
Name/address lookup uses domain service
Name servers are 255.255.255.255

Codes: UN - unknown, EX - expired, OK - OK, ?? - revalidate
       temp - temporary, perm - permanent
       NA - Not Applicable None - Not defined

Host           Port Flags   Age Type  Address(es)
dmz            None (perm, OK) 0  IP    209.10.10.1
ISP#
```

Now try to access the DMZ router by using the hostname:

```
ISP>telnet dmz
Trying 209.10.10.1 ...Open
User Access Verification

Password:
DMZ_Router>en
Password:
DMZ_Router#
```

SUCCESS!!! You are soooo amazing!!!!!

Network Device Backup and Recovery:

Often it takes days to configure routers on switches. During the subsequent months of operation, many changes are also made on the network devices. Unfortunately, regardless of the cost of the network device, there is always the chance for failure. Best practice for routers and switches is to print out the configurations of the device and store them in a safe place. Due to the nature of speed and changes in networks, however, the network administrator does not always have time to print out these configurations. In addition, a printout might not be the most practical method of assuring redundancy of network configurations because if the device had to be replaced all the commands to establish identical settings would have to be manually input. A far better option is using "Backup" and "Restore" options. These methods allow a replacement device to be installed in just a few days versus months of trial and error. If the replacement network device is the same model as the system which failed, the restoration to normal operation would only take minutes versus hours. In addition to safeguarding a copy of the configurations, the entire operating system can also be saved to be transferred to a replacement device. Below are two methods often used to save and restore the configurations on network devices:

- **Attachable Storage Unit (i.e. USB/Flashcard)** = On many network devices there is a USB port or a slot for a Flash Card. Using a terminal emulator and command line, it is possible to instruct the network device to save the configurations to the external memory storage unit. The following is the process for both saving and restoring configurations using external storage.
    1. **Backing up the Router Startup Configurations:**
        - ☐ Plug in the flashdrive.
        - ☐ **Type "copy startup-config flash:<BackupFilename>"**
        - ☐ Confirm the filename by hitting the "Enter" key.

    2. **To restore the configurations to a replacement router:**
        - ☐ **Type "copy flash: <BackupFilename> running-config"**
            - ➢ The router will take a few minutes and then load the restored settings which can now be displayed via hitting the "Enter" key followed by a "Show Run".
            - ➢ NOTE: These settings are not permanent and will be lost upon reboot of the router. To assure the settings are saved, perform a "Copy run start".

- **External Server or Network Device Backup** = Often times, there will be a server or storage area on a network in which router and switch configurations and even operating systems can be stored. When backing up an operating system, often the TCP/IP suite is utilized. Other times, perhaps only smaller files such as the running-configuration or the startup-configurations are stored. The following are some of the options for both saving and restoring configurations using an external backup device:

    3. **TCP/IP (Transmission Control Protocol/Internet Protocol)** = Often times, the devices which are to be backed up or restored are not in the same physical location in which the staff who need to work on it. In addition, maybe it is not economically feasible or safe to send a person to the location in which the router or switch is located. Using TCP/IP, it is possible to backup or restore a network device as long as it has a functioning IP address. The protocol is actually leveraging a different protocol to upload or download. The protocol called "FTP (File Transfer Protocol). Using TCP/IP the entire operating systems or individual startup files can be backed up and restored.

4. **TFTP (Trivial File Transfer Protocol)** = TFTP operates much like FTP except is has no error correction capabilities. When a file is uploaded or downloaded, there is no way to assure that the complete file has been transferred other than loading the operating system or actually reading the startup file (Called "Config.text). Another aspect of TFTP is that is can be extremely slow so it is primarily used for small configurations files although it does have the ability to transfer larger files at a slow speed. When using a TCP/IP or TFTP based network strategy, there is the need to have a computer which can receive the backup files. This computer traditionally has the name "TFTP Server". The name "Server" is misleading for the software is the actual server and can be installed on any small laptop or low powered computer. The command syntax for TCP/IP and TFTP backup and restore are identical. The following would be the process to backup the settings of the router:

- ☐ From the terminal emulator, ping the IP address of the TFTP server to assure it can be located.
- ☐ **Type "Copy run tftp** (This instructs the router to duplicate the "Running-Configurations" on a "TFTP" server.)
- ☐ Input the IP address of the TFTP server.
- ☐ Input the desired name the running-configuration will be called on the TFTP server (You can save the default name in the brackets if desired).
- ☐ Depending on the size of the file, after a few moments, the message "Transfer Complete" appears letting you know the transfer is complete.

- **Network Device Restore:**
  - ☐ Assure that network device has an IP address which can communicate with the TFTP Server (It is suggested that it is other than the actual IP address it will use for normal functioning.
  - ☐ From the terminal emulator, ping the IP address of the TFTP server to assure it can be located.
  - ☐ **Type "Copy tftp run** = This instructs the router to duplicate the "Running-Configurations" from a "TFTP" server to the network device's running-configuring.)
  - ☐ Input the IP address of the TFTP server.
  - ☐ Input the name of the running-configuration on the TFTP server.

☐ Confirm that the present running configurations should be overwritten by pressing "Enter".

☐ Depending on the size of the file, after a few moments, the message "Transfer Complete" appears letting you know the transfer is complete. After that message, press "Enter" and the new name on the network device will appear. To assure configuration, type "Show Run" to see all the new settings.

Chapter 19
Subnetting Concepts and Methods (Dividing Networks)

Subnetting Concepts and Methods (Dividing Networks):

The process of creating discrete sections inside of a larger network. Essentially, the different sections (Called "Subnets") are configured in a fashion which disallows each section to access the other. There are a number of reasons for this as in the following:

- **Security** = Creating a section of a network which has no access to outside resources which would hinder cyber and internet attacks.
- **Bandwidth Conservation** = Creating sections of networks so if a minor section is overwhelmed with network traffic, other more essential parts of the network will retain their optimal speed.
- **Special Use Devices** = Creating a "DMZ (Demilitarized Zone)" section of the network which contains all external facing and security servers such as firewalls, e-mail server, web filter, etc.

When there are subnets which need to function with other subnets, somewhere on the network there must exist a routing device of some type. Before discussion and attempting labs in subnetting, the following is a brief review about IP types:

- **Classfull IP addressing** = Primary method used on the Internet from 1981 to about early 1990's. Using the Classfull method, address spaces are divided into five address classes of "A, B and C" with two more such as "D" which is for "multicasting" and "E" reserved for military and experimental purposes. Below is an example of Classfull IP addressing:

Traditional Classfull IP Address Standards			
Class	Leading Octet	Subnet Mask	Maximum Hosts
A	0-127	255.0.0.0	16,777,214
B	128 - 191	255.255.0.0	65,534
C	192 - 223	255.255.255.0	254
D	224 - 239	Multicast	NA
E	240 - 247	Military Use	NA

Notes:
1) The "Leading Octet Ranges" display mathematical derivatives including reserved octets.
2) "Maximum Hosts" displays "Usable" hosts and not the pure mathematical derivatives.

- **Classless IP Addressing** = Due to the growth of the internet, there was a need to extend the range of available addressing. IPv6 is a method but the primary restriction to it is that older IPv4 devices could not communicate using IPv6. A solution to the decreasing number of available IPv4 addresses was produced with the implementation of VLSM and CIDR.

- o **Classless Internet Domain Routing (CIDR)** = When networks were developed, traffic was routed based on matching Classes (i.e., "A, "B", "C", etc) with a specific subnet mask ("255.0.0.0", "255.255.0.0" or "255.255.255.0"). Due to the increase in the number of devices, classfull IP addressing could not support the number of routes on the internet. IPv6 was created, but IPv4 will not understand routing from IPv6. Due to this challenge, programmers began to re-compile router operating systems in a manner which utilizes the "binary" form of numbers as opposed to the traditional method of "decimal" utilization. Because of this enhancement, subnet mask octets can include the following 9 numbers: 0, 128, 192, 224, 240, 248, 252, 254 and 255. With this method, the arrangement of "0's" or "1's" which are the "Binary" version of the decimal numbers dictate the following:

  - ☐ **Number of Networks**
  - ☐ **Number of Hosts**
  - ☐ **Routing Paths**

- o **Variable Length Subnet Masks (VLSM)** = Paralleling the utilization of CIDR, the method of documenting IP configurations has also evolved. Utilizing terms such as "Class A, B or C" or the traditional subnet masks such as "255.0.0.0, 255.255.0.0 and 255.255.255.0" are often replaced with the following class "C" CIDR examples:

Netmask Conversions		
Binary	Octet	CIDR
10000000	128	/25
11000000	192	/26
11100000	224	/27
11110000	240	/28
11111000	248	/29
11111100	252	/30
11111110	254	/31
11111111	255	NA (Or /32)
Assumes 1st three octets of "255.255.255.x"		

o As opposed to using decimal numbers as the subnet mask, the total amount of "binary" 1's in the subnet mask are added together and a two-character decimal number is used to reflect the subnet mask after the IP address and a "/" character (Often called a "forward slash"). Take the following for example:

  ❑ **Given CIDR subnet mask = 255.255.255.128**
    ➢ Binary format 11111111.11111111.11111111.10000000
    ➢ Count number of binary "1's" = 8+8+8+1 = 25 total.
    ➢ VLSM documentation = /25

Character-Types in Review:

In the field of network technology, there are various types of numbers which must be utilized to configure or communicate with different operating systems and devices. Some of the information on character types was mentioned in the early chapters but a quick review would be helpful to prepare for subnetting. Essentially, the type of characters which will be utilized in solving for hosts or networks would include the following:

- **Binary** = Binary characters are the foundation of computer and software technology. These characters are represented with either a "0" or a "1". Total numbers of combined characters have meaning in elements of instruction, storage and/or speed. Specific well-known combinations have the following names:
  o **Bit** = Single character as in "0" or "1".
  o **Nibble** = Four bits as in "0000" or "1111" or "0101".
  o **Byte** = Eight bits, or two "nibbles" as in "11110000"
  o Combinations of binary characters cause actions in software, hardware and identify devices. Often with programming, the two options for bits have specific meanings as in the following:
    ▪ 0 = off, no or false.
    ▪ 1 = on, yes or true.

- **Decimal** = The numbers are often seen on currency, thermostats and radios. The actual numbers are Zero thru Nine (0, 1, 2, 3, 4, 5, 6, 7, 8, 9). All numbers with two or more characters are still decimal numbers. In network technology, we often refer to decimal numbers when discussing an IP address, subnet mask or an "Octet".

- **Hexadecimal** = This type of numbering system includes decimal numbers and letters of the alphabet. All of the available decimal numbers are included. The following letters are included in this system (A, B, C, D, E, and F). Computers cannot manipulate "double character" numbers (i.e., "12" or "14"). To compensate for this, letters are used to represent two-digit numbers. The letter "A" equal the decimal number "10". The letter "B" represents the decimal number "11". Below is a diagram which displays hexadecimal numbers as well as binary and decimal.

Network Related Numbers Conversion		
Decimal	Hexadecimal	Binary
0	0	0000
1	1	0001
2	2	0010
3	3	0011
4	4	0100
5	5	0101
6	6	0110
7	7	0111
8	8	1000
9	9	1001
10	A	1010
11	B	1011
12	C	1100
13	D	1101
14	E	1110
15	F	1111

- **Octet** = These appear as any one of the 4 decimal numbers separated by periods within an IP address or a subnet mask. Each of the decimal numbers can range from 0 to 255. Although the numbers are in decimal format, understand that it is actually the binary versions of these numbers which are used. It is often difficult to remember large strings of binary digits. The decimal appearance is to assist the eye of humans to perceive and remember the numbers. In the field of network technology, we often utilize one type number to represent a different type of number. This is normally because it would be difficult for the human mind to "memorize" collections of specific types of numbers. IP addresses are just one example. Below is a graphic which displays how decimal addresses are actually representing a string of binary numbers:

IP Address to Binary Example			
172	16	10	5
10101100	00010000	00001010	00000101

Subnet Mask to Binary Example			
255	255	255	0
11111111	11111111	11111111	00000000

Subnetting Process:

In order to pass many Cisco, Microsoft and CompTIA examinations, it will be required to be able to answer questions related to subnetting. All answers must be derived manually. No calculators are allowed. For this reason, it is important that a network technician develop a method for addressing subnet questions which is both accurate and fast. In addition, the method must be able to answer any of SIX different subnetting questions, the answers of which are all directly related. The following are the questions which may have to be addressed:

- **Network ID** = What section of the IP address range identifies each network?
- **First Available** = What is the first IP address on a specific network which a device can use?
- **Broadcast** = What IP address on the network will be used for devices to announce themselves?
- **Last Available** = What is the last IP address on a specific network which a device can use?
- **Range or ("Hosts")** = How many devices can exist in a section of a network?
- **Networks** = How many networks will be available?

The questions are listed above in an order which might make solving them easier. For network technicians with highly developed skill in math and understanding of mathematical formulas for evaluating "Powers of 2 (i.e., "2^4") will have less to learn, but anyone else may find subnetting challenging. In addition, due to the time limitations of certification examinations, utilizing math processes may require too much time. Due to these reasons, there is a process which uses a "Subnetting Table" which allows swift resolution to the above six subnetting questions. Please review the graphics below which will be discussed and utilized for upcoming labs:

Subnetting Table									
(H-2)	4	8	16	32	64	128	256	512	1024

Netmask Conversions		
Binary	Octet	CIDR
10000000	128	/25
11000000	192	/26
11100000	224	/27
11110000	240	/28
11111000	248	/29
11111100	252	/30
11111110	254	/31
11111111	255	NA (Or /32)

Subnetting: Solving for Hosts:

For our exercises, we will be using subnetting using CIDR standards. Using the "Subnetting Table" only requires basic mathematics and formula (Position) substitution. This means that some numbers are only "Indicators", "Placeholders" or "Symbols" of meaning. The following are two of examples:
- Binary "0's" have the meaning of "Hosts/Nodes/Clients".
- Binary "1's" have the meaning of "Networks/Subnets".

The scale in the subnetting table is used to both identify hosts or subnets by pointing to a particular number which is isolated using the binary characters in the subnet mask. The more information required, the more data will be provided in the original question. In addition, the answer of the question can take on the form of an IP address, a decimal network mask, a CIDR mask (Also called "Slash Notation"), etc. Take the following example:

- You have 13 subnets and a computer with the IP address of 172.16.20.44. What is required to derive a subnet with 22 hosts? Answer 255.255.255.224 (or /27)

Yep. The answer was that easy. I just used one finger on one hand! Really! Before we try a question, let's look at the process. When processing a problem, it is very important to break the question down into all of its parts. Do not attempt to process the entire question all at once. Below, I have segmented the question. Let's evaluate some of the parts of the question:

- You have 13 subnets and a computer with the IP address of 172.16.20.44. **WHAT IS REQUIRED TO DERIVE A SUBNET WITH 22 HOSTS?** Answer 255.255.255.224 (or /27)

Many of the parts are not needed for the answer. In this situation, only the BLACK UPPERCASE section is required with the question part requiring 22 hosts support. The process continues,.....

In order to create subnet sections, it is required to manipulate the subnet mask. In reality, the question is asking "What subnet mask would allow 22 hosts?" When addressing this question, it is important to know that your answer will not render exactly 22 hosts. In network subnetting, your answer will more than likely arrive at a number "Close to, but not below" the number you are evaluating.

All the answers are closer to the term "At least and includes ......". We will use the subnetting table which has static numbers in specific blocks which never change. When asked a specific number, you will find the number provided by the scale which includes the number just above and closest to the number specified in the question. This will also be the case later when working with finding a number of networks. Let us continue with the process. Using the scale, you must locate where the desired number would fall. Using your finger, you see that the number 22 falls between "16" and "32". In this process, we must locate the number which includes or is just above the number specified in the problem. Here we see that "32" is the only number which includes 22. The number 16 would be too small.

Subnetting Table									
(H-2)	4	8	16	32	64	128	256	512	1024
X	X	X	X	X					

Due to this, although the specified number was "22" the derived answer will actually allow 32 hosts on each subnet. The number "32" was not requested in the question, however. It is just part of the process to find the final answer. In addition, this is a mathematical answer. It cannot be used by the network engineer. There are a few physical rules which will modify this number again.

On any given network, there are some "special use" numbers. These numbers are often used to divide or describe networks on documentation. These numbers are recorded and used for reference in a number of different ways, none of which are network communication. For this reason, they are never actually used on any devices. When solving for hosts, we must subtract "two" from whatever number we drop on to reflect these unused number. Because we dropped on the number "32", we must subtract two (hosts) which gives us a new number of 30. Again, this answer was not requested, but it appears in any case. Let us continue to get the answer we are attempting to derive.

Using the subnet table, we have to count the number of value spaces moving from "left to right (Starting from "H-2")." Until we are under the identified number of "32"

Subnetting Table									
(H-2)	4	8	16	32	64	128	256	512	1024
X	X	X	X	X					
0	0	0	0	0					

As was determined before, we have stopped at the listed number of "32 (Which renders the result of 30)" which is a total of "five" spaces from the left. Remember this number. Now we move to the table which displays "Netmask Conversions" of subnet mask numbers. When we are using the table, we now substitute binary zeros (0) for the total number of spaces we moved from right-to-left. The subnetting table below displays the process:

Subnetting Table									
(H-2)	4	8	16	32	64	128	256	512	1024
X	X	X	X	X					
0	0	0	0	0					

With this scale, we have to remember the number of spaces we moved from left to right on the previous scale. That number was "five". In one of our legends, it is illustrated that the binary character "0" would be used for the determination of hosts. Using the netmask conversion scale, select the binary string which has only "five zero's" moving from "right-to-left".

Netmask Conversions		
Binary	Octet	CIDR
10000000	128	/25
11000000	192	/26
11100000	224	/27
11110000	240	/28
11111000	248	/29
11111100	252	/30
11111110	254	/31
11111111	255	NA (Or /32)

When solving for hosts (Or even subnetworks), the question is primarily asking for the appropriate subnet mask to use.

Associated with the binary string "11100000" is "224" in decimal format. In this scenario, the answer must be offered in a netmask format requiring octets. In the process, we have used a single octet moving from "right-to-left" leaving us three leading octets remaining. If octets are not used in the problem solving, they are assumed to be "255". The final result would be a subnet mask of 255.255.255.224 (Or: "/27" in CIDR) to allow 22 hosts with the potential of up to 30. Let us attempt another "host related" problem:

- You have a network with 13 subnets. If a computer is on the network with the IP address of 172.16.0.0, what is required to make sure that subnet can **SUPPORT 800 HOSTS?**

Notice that a big change is the number of hosts and the displayed IP address. To answer this question, you will do the same process as before but add a step. As in the last problem question, many of the parts are not needed for the answer. In this situation, only the **BOLD UPPERCASE** section is required with the question part requiring supporting 800 hosts. The question is asking "What subnet mask should all the computers on that subnet have to assure there are 800 hosts?" As before, the process continues,…..

We are now looking for a number on the "Subnet Table" which is "At least and includes 800". Using the scale, you must locate where the desired number (800) would fall. Using your finger, you see that the number 800 falls between "512" and "1024".

Subnetting Table									
(H-2)	4	8	16	32	64	128	256	512	1024
X	X	X	X	X	X	X	X	X	X

The number 512 would be too little hosts. Due to this, although the specified number was "800" the derived answer will actually allow 1024 IP's on each subnet. The number "1024" was not requested in the question, however. It is just part of the process to find the final answer. Remember that this a mathematical answer. It cannot be used by the network engineer. Due to the process of network documentation and protocol communication, we have to make allowance for the "Special Use" numbers. Since we are solving for "hosts" we must subtract "2" from the number we are using. Since our located number is "1024", after subtracting "2" we have a final resulting number of 1022 hosts that will be available on the network although only 800 was requested. Again, with subnetting, the goal is not to get the exact number but to locate the number including and just above the number specified in the question. Now that we have a number, we must create the appropriate subnet mask to support our number.

Using the subnetting table, we have to count the number of value spaces moving from the "1024" back down to "H-2".

Subnetting Table									
(H-2)	4	8	16	32	64	128	256	512	1024
X	X	X	X	X	X	X	X	X	X
0	0	0	0	0	0	0	0	0	0

As was determined before, using the listed number of "1024" as a starting point results in moving a total of "10" spaces from right-to-left. Now simply write down the number of spaces using 10 zeros. Special notice here,…you may have noticed that the answer we will derive will include more than eight characters. In this answer, you will actually use the "last two" octets in the subnet mask. Let's continue,….

Moving from "right-to-left", count up to the number of space moved and place a period (.) after the "eighth" space. The first 8 spaces you moved is the binary form of the "fourth" octet. Although not listed, eight binary zeros equal the decimal "0". You notice you have two binary zeros ("0") remaining. These characters will become the last two binary characters in the third octet. Remember, octets have a total of eight binary characters. If they are not "0's", then they must be "1's". Add six binary "1's" to the left-hand portion of the remaining two zeros which completes the requirements for the third octet. The result is two octets.

Move to the table which displays netmask conversions of subnet mask numbers. With this problem, we will look for the binary match for each octet. Again, the section which has "8" binary zeros converts to "0" in decimal. The octet which has "11111100" converts to "252" in decimal.

Netmask Conversions		
Binary	Octet	CIDR
10000000	128	/25
11000000	192	/26
11100000	224	/27
11110000	240	/28
11111000	248	/29
11111100	252	/30
11111110	254	/31
11111111	255	NA (Or /32)
Assumes 1st three octets of "255.255.255.x"		

The resulting decimal string resulting from conversion would be "252.0" in decimal format. In this scenario, the host must be offered in a netmask format requiring four octets. In the process, we have used two octets moving from "right-to-left" leaving us two leading octets remaining. If octets are not used in the solving the problem, they are assumed to be "255". The final result would be a subnet mask of 255.255.252.0 (Or "/22") to allow the 800 hosts with the potential of up to 1022.

Go ahead and attempt the following problems to practice:
- You have a network with 11 subnets. If a computer is on the network with the IP address of 172.16.22.0, what is required to make sure that subnet can support 80 hosts?
- You have a network with 22 subnets. If a computer is on the network with the IP address of 182.16.22.0, what is required to make sure that subnet can support 14 hosts?
- You have a network with 35 subnets. If a computer is on the network with the IP address of 198.16.22.0, what is required to make sure that subnet can support 258 hosts?

Subnetting: Solving for Networks:

In addition to questions concerning hosts, subnetting question also include locating numbers of subnets. We can use the same methods which requires a subnet mask to be created. There will be small modifications as in the following:

- There must be IP address information in the question.
- Remember classfull IP addressing in the process.
- We will concentrate on binary "1's" in this process.
- The significant spaces will move from "left-to-right".

Let's walk thru the process of solving for a subnet:

- On a network with a network address of 191.16.25.0, what is required to make sure that SUBNET CAN SUPPORT 10 NETWORKS?   Answer = 255.255.255.240 or /28

In this scenario, we need first use the BOLD BLACK area then we will use the UPPERCASE BLACK. We will use the same subnet table used to find hosts. Find the number which includes or is one step greater than "10". You notice the number which must be selected appears between "8" and "16".

Subnetting Table									
(H-2)	4	8	16	32	64	128	256	512	1024
X	X	X	X						

Based on the method, we will use the "16". When solving for subnets, no numbers are subtracted. The process continues by counting the number of spaces from "right-to-left" the "16" is from the far left. It can be noticed that there are 4 spaces which were moved. Now we need to start adding some more processes for subnetting. When solving for networks, the rules for "Classfull subnetting" must be referenced. Specific rules are which IP address class requires which subnet mask. Refer to the chart below:

Traditional Classfull IP Address Standards			
Class	Leading Octet	Subnet Mask	Maximum Hosts
A	0-127	255.0.0.0	16,777,214
B	128 - 191	255.255.0.0	65,534
C	192 - 223	255.255.255.0	254
D	224 - 239	Multicast	NA
E	240 - 247	Military Use	NA

Notes:
1) The "Leading Octet Ranges" display mathematical derivatives including reserved octets.
2) "Maximum Hosts" displays "Usable" hosts and not the pure mathematical derivatives.

Notice the IP address in the question is "Class B" which would normally have "255.255.0.0" as the subnet mask. Using the method in this text, we associate any octets which has "255" in it to be "Unchangeable". Any subnet octet which has "0" in it can be utilized to create subnetworks. In this case, the "0's" in the last two octets. Refer to the following chart:

Subnetting Process Related to Classfull Addresses:		
Leading Octet	Class	Netmask Creation Sections
0-127	A	255.0.0.0
128-191	B	255.255.0.0
192 - 223	C	255.255.255.0

The remainder of problem is addressed in the following manner:
- Traditional IP Address = 192.16.25.0
- Associated Traditional Subnet Mask = 255.255.255.0
- Non-Changing section (First Three Octets) = 255.255.255
- Area for network creation in decimal (Last Octet) = 0

As mentioned earlier, when solving for networks, we will be utilizing the binary "1's" to define our subnets. We will replace the binary "0's" in the octet for creation with binary "1's" moving from "left-to-right" as in the following manner:

- Octet area for subnet creation in binary form = Last Octet of "00000000"
- Total number of spaces moved on subnet table = 4 total.

Subnetting Table									
(H-2)	4	8	16	32	64	128	256	512	1024
X	X	X	X						
1	1	1	1						

- Convert the number of moved spaces into a binary value = 1111
- Add binary "0's" in the creation octet after the last binary "1" to create a full binary octet = 11110000.
- On the netmask conversion table, locate the decimal number associated with the binary octet found:

Netmask Conversions		
Binary	Octet	CIDR
10000000	128	/25
11000000	192	/26
11100000	224	/27
11110000	240	/28
11111000	248	/29
11111100	252	/30
11111110	254	/31
11111111	255	NA (Or /32)
Assumes 1st three octets of "255.255.255.x"		

- Convert the new binary combination to decimal and replace the section for creation in the original subnet mask = 255.255.255.240

Using the combination of 192.16.25.0 network address for all IP's combined with the subnet mask of "255.255.255.240" (Or "/28") allows the support of the requested number networks.

Let's try another:
- On a network with a network address of 199.22.45.0, what is required to make sure that SUBNET CAN SUPPORT 60 NETWORKS? Answer = 255.255.255.252 or /30

We will use the same "Subnet Table" as with other problems. Find the number which includes or is one step greater than "60".

Subnetting Table									
(H-2)	4	8	16	32	64	128	256	512	1024
X	X	X	X	X	X				

You notice the number which must be selected appears between "32" and "64". Based on the method, we will use the "64". When solving for subnets, no number are subtracted. The process continues by counting the number of spaces from "right-to-left" the "64" is from the far left. It can be noticed that there are 6 spaces which were moved. Now we need to start adding some more processes for subnetting. When solving to networks, the rules for "Classfull subnetting" must be referenced. Specific rules are which IP address class requires which subnet mask. Refer to the chart below:

Traditional Classfull IP Address Standards			
Class	Leading Octet	Subnet Mask	Maximum Hosts
A	0-127	255.0.0.0	16,777,214
B	128 - 191	255.255.0.0	65,534
C	192 - 223	255.255.255.0	254
D	224 - 239	Multicast	NA
E	240 - 247	Military Use	NA

Notes:
  1) The "Leading Octet Ranges" display mathematical derivatives including reserved octets.
  2) "Maximum Hosts" displays "Usable" hosts and not the pure mathematical derivatives.

Notice the IP address in the question is "Class C" which would normally have "255.255.255.0" as the subnet mask. Using the method in this text, we associate any octets which has "255" in it as "not-to-be-changed". Any octet which has "0" in it can be utilized to create subnetworks. In this case, the "0" is in the last or fourth octet. Refer to the following chart:

The remainder of problem is addressed via the following:
  • Traditional IP Address = 199.22.45.0
  • Associated Traditional Subnet Mask = 255.255.255.0
  • Non-Changing section (First Three Octets) = 255.255.255
  • Area for network creation in decimal (Last Octet) = 0

As mentioned earlier, when solving for networks, we will be utilizing the binary "1's" to define our subnets. We will replace the binary "0's" in the octet for creation with binary "1's" moving from "left-to-right" as in the following manner:

Subnetting Table										
(H-2)	4	8	16	32	64	128	256	512	1024
X	X	X	X	X	X				
1	1	1	1	1	1				

- Original Creation octet binary form = 00000000
- Total number of spaces moved on Subnet Table = 6 total.
- Convert the number of moved spaces into a binary value = 111111
- Add binary "0's" in the creation octet after the last binary "1" to create a binary octet = 11111100.
- Using the netmask conversion table, find which is most similar to the binary value.

Netmask Conversions		
Binary	Octet	CIDR
10000000	128	/25
11000000	192	/26
11100000	224	/27
11110000	240	/28
11111000	248	/29
11111100	252	/30
11111110	254	/31
11111111	255	NA (Or /32)

Assumes 1st three octets of "255.255.255.x"

- Convert the new binary combination to decimal and replace the section for creation in the original subnet mask = 255.255.255.252

Just like with our examples with isolating the number of hosts, often times we will be working with other classes of subnet masks such as a "class B". The same charts and methods apply. Let's look at the same question with an IP address in the question of 179.22.45.0

Notice the IP address in the question is "Class B" which would normally have "255.255.0.0" as the subnet mask. Using the method in this text, we associate any octets which has "255" in it as "not-to-be-changed". Any octet which has "0" in it can be utilized to create subnetworks. In this case, the "0's" are in the last two, or third and fourth octet. Refer to the following chart:

Subnetting Process Related to Classfull Addresses:		
Leading Octet	Class	Netmask Creation Sections
0-127	A	255.0.0.0
128-191	B	255.255.0.0
192 - 223	C	255.255.255.0

The remainder of problem is addressed via the following:
- Traditional IP Address = 179.22.45.0
- Associated Traditional Subnet Mask = 255.255.0.0
- Non-Changing section (First Two Octets) = 255.255
- Area for network creation in decimal (Last Two Octets) = 0.0

As mentioned earlier, when solving for networks, we will be utilizing the binary "1's" to define our subnets. We will replace the binary "0's" in the subnet section for creation with binary "1's" moving from "left-to-right" as in the following manner:

- Original creation octets binary form = 00000000.00000000
- Total number of spaces moved on Subnet Table= 6 total.

Subnetting Table									
(H-2)	4	8	16	32	64	128	256	512	1024
X	X	X	X	X	X				
1	1	1	1	1	1				

- Convert the number of moved spaces into a binary value = 111111
- Replace the "0's" in the creation octets with binary "1's" moving from "left-to-right" = 11111100.00000000
- Locate the modified octets in the Netmask Conversion Table (Remember that eight binary "0's" equal a "decimal" number "8".):

Netmask Conversions		
Binary	Octet	CIDR
10000000	128	/25
11000000	192	/26
11100000	224	/27
11110000	240	/28
11111000	248	/29
11111100	252	/30
11111110	254	/31
11111111	255	NA (Or /32)
Assumes 1st three octets of "255.255.255.x"		

- Convert the new binary combination to decimal and replace the section for creation in the original subnet mask = 255.255.252.0 (Or "/22)

Try some of the following problems:
  - On a network with a network address of 129.35.58.0, what is required to make sure that subnet can support 20 networks?
  - On a network with a network address of 179.42.65.0, what is required to make sure that subnet can support 80 networks?
  - On a network with a network address of 200.2.85.0, what is required to make sure that subnet can support 30 networks?
  - On a network with a network address of 114.68.47.0, what is required to make sure that subnet can support 72 networks?
  - On a network with a network address of 199.22.45.0, what is required to make sure that subnet can support 55 networks?

Complex Subnetting Questions:
Often times, a question will require you to find two or more of the six possible answers. Take the following, for example. The important elements are highlighted:

  - A computer on a network has the IP address of 199.22.45.88, what is required to make sure that subnet can support 29 networks with 6 hosts on each? Answer = 255.255.255.248 or /29

The question above requires all of the processes we used for previous subnetting problems. With this combination subnet calculation, it is recommended that you break the questions into the following sequence of operations abbreviated as H, N, S:

1. **H = Hosts**
2. **N = Networks**
3. **S = Subnet mask**

When solving this type of question, the following questions are the elements needed:

- What would be a possible subnet mask for 6 hosts (closet number would be 8)?
- Would the mask allow 29 networks (Closest number would be 32)?
- Does the traditional mask for the given IP (199.22.45.88) support the developed subnet mask if it was classfull (255.255.255.0)?

Let's work the problem:

- To get 6 hosts:
    1. Use subnet table to move up to "8" which results in a usable total of "6".
    2. Count the spaces up to and including "8" which equals "3 spaces".

Subnetting Table									
(H-2)	4	8	16	32	64	128	256	512	1024
X	X	X							
0	0	0							

3. The "host indicator" is the binary "0" so 3 spaces results in "000".
4. Add binary "1's" from the most left binary "0's" resulting in a binary octet of "11111000".
5. On the netmask conversion table, locate entry with "11111000" from right-to-left which is "248".

Netmask Conversions		
Binary	Octet	CIDR
10000000	128	/25
11000000	192	/26
11100000	224	/27
11110000	240	/28
11111000	248	/29
11111100	252	/30
11111110	254	/31
11111111	255	NA (Or /32)
Assumes 1st three octets of "255.255.255.x"		

- We have found a way to support the hosts, now we make sure the same mask can support the networks. First we remember that binary "1's" are "Network Indicators".
    1. Using the subnet table, find the number just larger than "29" which is the value slot for "32".
    2. We count the number of spaces from the value 32 to "H-2" from "right-to-left".
    3. We notice that we moved a total of "5" value spaces. Now we check to see if the original octet binary number has the same amount of binary "1's" in the octet going from "right-to-left".
    4. Double-check the "netmask conversion" table to assure that the same subnet was found compared to the subnet mask used for creating the number of network:

Subnetting Table									
(H-2)	4	8	16	32	64	128	256	512	1024
X	X	X	X	X					
1	1	1	1	1					

5. We can see that the subnet mask derived in both processes is identical. We can now be assured that the appropriate subnet mask would be "255.255.255.248"

Let's Try another:
- A computer on a network has the IP address of 201.16.33.52, what is required to make sure that subnet can support 6 networks with 30 hosts on each?   Answer = 255.255.255.224 or /27

The question above requires all of the processes we used for previous subnetting problems. With this combination subnet calculation, it is recommended that you break the questions into the following sequence of operations abbreviated as H, N, S:
1. H = Hosts
2. N = Networks
3. S = Subnet mask

When solving this type of problem, the following questions are the elements needed:
- What would be a possible subnet mask for 30 hosts (closet number would be 32)?

- What is the mask to allow 6 networks (Closest number would be 8)?
- Does the traditional mask for the given IP (201.16.33.52) support the developed subnet mask if it was classfull (255.255.255.0)?

Let's work the problem:
- To get 30 hosts:
  1. Use subnet table and find to move up to "32" which results in a usable total of "30".
  2. Count the spaces up to and including "32" which equals "5 spaces".
  3. The "host indicator" is the binary "0" so 5 spaces x "0" displays as "00000".

Subnetting Table									
(H-2)	4	8	16	32	64	128	256	512	1024
X	X	X	X	X					
0	0	0	0	0					

  4. On Decimal-to-Binary chart locate entry with "00000" from right-to-left which is "224"

Netmask Conversions		
Binary	Octet	CIDR
10000000	128	/25
11000000	192	/26
11100000	224	/27
11110000	240	/28
11111000	248	/29
11111100	252	/30
11111110	254	/31
11111111	255	NA (Or /32)

Assumes 1st three octets of "255.255.255.x"

  5. "224" in binary displays three "1's" (111).
  6. Binary "1's" are "Network Indicators".

7. Using the Subnet Table, moving from left-to-right, a total of three spaces results at a destination of 8, which is appropriate to support 6 networks.

Subnetting Table									
(H-2)	4	8	16	32	64	128	256	512	1024
X	X	X							
1	1	1							

8. With the above process completed, the correct subnet mask would be "255.255.255.224"

The process of finding hosts or networks will work regardless of which octet changes. Let's Try one more problem using a different subnet type:

- A computer on a network has the IP address of 172.16.33.52, what is required to make sure that subnet can support 60 networks with 1000 hosts on each? Answer = 255.255.252.0 or /22

Pay special attention to the 1st octet. The number "172" would place the network into a "Class B" subnet which normally display as "255.255.0.0".

Traditional Classfull IP Address Standards			
Class	Leading Octet	Subnet Mask	Maximum Hosts
A	0-127	255.0.0.0	16,777,214
B	128 - 191	255.255.0.0	65,534
C	192 - 223	255.255.255.0	254
D	224 - 239	Multicast	NA
E	240 - 247	Military Use	NA

Notes:
1) The "Leading Octet Ranges" display mathematical derivatives including reserved octets.
2) "Maximum Hosts" displays "Usable" hosts and not the pure mathematical derivatives.

In this case, anything which is "255" in the netmask will not be changed. This leaves the last two octets "0.0" to be open for host and network separation.

Subnetting Process Related to Classfull Addresses:		
Leading Octet	Class	Netmask Creation Sections
0-127	A	255.0.0.0
128-191	B	255.255.0.0
192 - 223	C	255.255.255.0

Also pay special attention to the number of hosts requested. It requires "1000" hosts. The highest number of host possible from any single octet is "254". Because this problem requires more hosts, it will be necessary to use binary spaces from more than one octet. Essentially, we begin to use bits from the octet furthest right and work our way to the left. When you start these types of problems, ignore the periods (".") between the octets. We will re-add them later.

The question above requires all of the processes we used for previous subnetting problems. With this combination subnet calculation, it is recommended that you break the questions into the following sequence of operations (H,N,S = Hosts, then Networks, then Subnet mask):

- What would be a possible subnet mask for 1000 hosts (closet number would be 1024)?
- What mask allows 60 networks (Closest number would be 64)?
- Does the traditional mask for the given IP (172.16.33.52) support the developed subnet mask if it was classfull (255.255.0.0)?

Let's work the problem:
- To get 1000 hosts:
    1. Use Subnet table to move up to "1024" which results in a usable total of "1022" usable hosts which supports the desired number of 1000 hosts..
    2. Count the spaces up to and including "1024" which equals "10 spaces".
    3. Write out 10 zeros from right-to-left.

Subnetting Table									
(H-2)	4	8	16	32	64	128	256	512	1024
X	X	X	X	X	X	X	X	X	X
0	0	0	0	0	0	0	0	0	0

4. Count the zeros from right-to-left and place a period "." to the left of the eighth zero. This should give you a result which looks like "00.00000"
5. Add enough binary "1's" to the left of the zeros closet to the period "." to render a total of eight binary characters "11111100". This will leave the total binary display as follows "11111100.00000000"
6. Although the Netmask Conversion table does not display it, remember "00000000" from right-to-left equals a decimal zero ("0")
7. On the Netmask Conversion table, locate the entry with "11111100" from right-to-left which is "252".

Netmask Conversions		
Binary	Octet	CIDR
10000000	128	/25
11000000	192	/26
11100000	224	/27
11110000	240	/28
11111000	248	/29
11111100	252	/30
11111110	254	/31
11111111	255	NA (Or /32)
Assumes 1st three octets of "255.255.255.x"		

8. This binary string of character will be converted to decimal format as in "252.0".
9. The "252.0" is to be added to the classfull netmask of "255.255" which results in "255.255.252.0".
10. The "host indicators" are the binary "0", so 10 spaces x "0" displays as "0000000000".
11. Binary "1's" after the classfull netmask are "Network Indicators".
12. There are a total of six binary "1's" after the classfull netmask (11111100).
13. Using the Subnet Table, moving from left-to-right a total of six spaces results at a destination of 64, which is appropriate to support 64 networks.
14. With the above process completed, the correct subnet mask would be "255.255.252.0"

Early in this chapter, we discussed the idea that there were a number of questions which involves subnetting. In review, the following are the questions which may have to be addressed:

- **Network ID** = What section of the IP address range identifies each network?
- **First Available** = What is the first IP address on a specific network which a device can use?
- **Broadcast** = What IP address on the network will be used for devices to announce themselves?
- **Last Available** = What is the last IP address on a specific network which a device can use?
- **Hosts** = How many devices can exist in a section of a network?
- **Networks** = How many networks will be available?

Working with the earlier subnetting questions, we address the last two items but we still must be able to derive the following:

- **Network ID** = What section of the IP address range identifies each network?
- **First Available** = What is the first IP address on a specific network which a device can use?
- **Broadcast** = What IP address on the network will be used for devices to announce themselves?
- **Last Available** = What is the last IP address on a specific network which a device can use?

The process for solving the subnetting question below will require the use of the subnetting table of the method chart as below:

Subnetting Table									
(H-2)	4	8	16	32	64	128	256	512	1024

The primary section you will use will be the octet which allows the creation of the subnets. This section is often derived from a previous question or may actually appear in the text of the questions. Using a previous problem for example:

- A computer on a network has the IP address of 201.16.33.52, what is required to make sure that subnet can support 6 networks with 30 hosts on each? Answer = 255.255.255.224 or /27

We will not process the entire problem, we just needed to get the answer which can be written as "255.255.255.224" or "/27". The section we will need to answer the remaining four questions will be the octet which allows the creation of the subnets. In this scenario, we will use the last octet which is "224".

To begin the process, we will use the number 256 as our base subnet number. This is due to using pure math and the powers of "2", this is the highest number for any given octet. After we find out the value of the octet used to isolate hosts or networks, we will subtract that number from "256" which will provide us our answers. Take the following for example:

- Base number for subnet ranges = 256
- Derived/Given Subnet number to subtract from base = -224
- Resulting number from subtraction = 32
- The "32" instantly gives us two answers which are identical:
  - Total number of hosts possible on each network = 32 hosts
  - 2nd network ID = 32

The following are the examples of all the networks. Begin with the real starting 4th octet of "0" and the subsequent networks will follow in groups of "32 as in the following:
- First Network = 201.16.33.0
- Second Network = 201.16.33.32
- Third Network = 201.16.33.64
- Fourth Network = 201.16.33.96
- Fifth Network = 201.16.33.128
- Sixth Network = 201.16.33.160
- Seventh Network = 201.16.33.192
- Eight Network = 201.16.33.224
- END

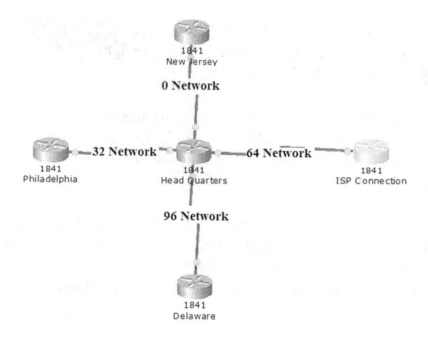

When subnetting for range, when you find a host address which matches your netmask, you have arrived at the end of your network. Using the numbers we derived from the base number subtraction, we can get the following answers. Using the first subnet, let's answer the following questions:

- **Network ID** = What section of the IP address range identifies each network?
  - o **Answer** = This is the number we have developed from subtracting the netmask number (224) from the base number (256) which give us "32". The Subnet ID is the last octet due to subtracting the derived subnet mask octet as in the following sections highlighted in BOLD BLACK:
    - ☐ First network starts = 201.16.33.0
    - ☐ Second network starts = 201.16.33.32
    - ☐ Third network starts = 201.16.33.64
    - ☐ Fourth network starts = 201.16.33.96
    - ☐ Fifth network starts = 201.16.33.128
    - ☐ Sixth network starts = 201.16.33.160
    - ☐ Seventh network starts = 201.16.33.192
    - ☐ Eighth network starts = 201.16.33.224 (Stop here!)

  - o Each network has a specific range of IP addresses. Different subnets cannot communicate with others unless there exists a router which connects the different networks. Within each network, there are names associated with specific IP addresses such as:

- **First Available** = What is the first IP address on a specific network which a device can use?
- **Broadcast** = What IP address on the network will be used for devices to announce themselves?
- **Last Available** = What is the last IP address on a specific network which a device can use?

o Let us evaluate the 3rd subnet which begins as 201.16.33.64:

- **First Available** = After using the subnetting process, we found that the third network begins with the network ID of 201.16.33.64. Whichever IP represents the network ID is never used. It is used for labeling and references purposes on documents. This results in the first IP address which can be placed on a device to be whichever IP appears after the Network ID. We refer to this as the "First Available". In this scenario, the first usable IP would be "201.16.33.65".

- **Broadcast Address** = This would be the address which appears just before the next network. In this scenario, the next, or fourth network, would start with the IP address of "201.16.33.96". The address just before the fourth network ID would be "201.16.33.95" which makes it the broadcast for the third network. As stated earlier, the broadcast address is not placed on any device but it will automatically be used by all nodes to advertise their existence on that subnet.

- **Last Available** = Once we have located the broadcast address, we can easily identify the last IP address from that subnet which can be utilized on a host or node. The last available will be just before the broadcast for that particular network. Since our network (The third network of "201.16.33.64) has a broadcast of "201.16.33.95" then the last available would be "201.16.33.94".

o Let's evaluate the information for the sixth subnet:

- **Sixth network starts** = 201.16.33.160
- **First Available (After Network ID)** = 201.16.33.161
- **Broadcast (Before Next network ID)** = 201.16.33.191
- **Last Available (Before Broadcast)** = 201.16.33.190

Try a few of the exercises below:

- A computer on a network has the IP address of 151.20.55.13, what is required to make sure that subnet can support 12 networks with 14 hosts on each?

- A computer on a network has the IP address of 192.17.101.50, what is required to make sure that subnet can support 4 networks with 20 hosts on each?

- A computer on a network has the IP address of 189.20.55.13, what is required to make sure that subnet can support 24 networks with 14 hosts on each?

- A computer on a network has the IP address of 154.90.85.16, what is required to make sure that subnet can support 60 networks with 100 hosts on each?

Chapter 20
IP Version 6 Concepts

IP Version 6 Concepts:

Before attempting to understand and manipulate IPv6, let's do a quick review of why it exists. Originally, IPv4 was designed and supported by the department of defense (DOD) as a method to support worldwide military defense base communications in the event traditional means of communications (i.e., radio, television and telephone) were to be disrupted. When the decision was made, only military installations were connected to the internet. As time progressed, more organizations, businesses and entities purchased an "internet" presence such as airports, universities and businesses. The increased number on the internet (Or what was known as the "World Wide Web" at that time) began to exhaust the available number of IPv4 addresses which is limited to about 4 billion. Due to the need to expand the numbering system of the internet, programmers and engineers designed a new version of node addressing entitled IPv6. This method utilized 128 bits instead of 32. It is theorized that IPv6 will be able to support over 340 "undecillion" ip addresses (Yes, this is a true number. It is the digit "1" followed by 36 "zeros") required for the growing internet for a significant amount of years. There is one caveat to the implementation of IPv6 however and that is universal compatibility.

IPv6 is totally backwards compatible which means that it understands IPv4 communications. The reverse, however is not the case. IPv4 devices do not understand communications from IPv6 devices or networks. When there is a need for a IPv4 network to understand communications from an IPv6 network, there must be a "bridging" device or software which converts between the different networks. Some of the technologies include " Network Address Translation-Protocol Translation (NAT-PT)", "Dual Stack Application Level Gateways (DS-ALG)", "6to4 Dynamic Tunneling" and many other methods. The particulars of the conversion methods listed are beyond the scope of this text but require due mention for conversational purposes.

Although IPv6 is a stable and robust method of node addressing, it by itself does not address the lack of communications to strictly IPv4 networks. There are millions of IPv4 networks in existence which work perfectly fine. It would be financially counter-productive to replace working equipment to allow for communications with new networks which only use IPv6. Programmers and engineers created an additional method of IP addressing called "Classless Internet Domain Routing (CIDR) with "Variable Length Subnet Masks (VLSM) to bridge the communication problem as well as compensate for the decreasing number of IP addresses which can be offered to internet based participants.

Even with the advent of CIDR and VLSM, IPv6 is slated to be the preferred method of node addressing for the foreseeable future.

IP Version 6 Format and Structure:

The display of an IP version 6 address uses what is known as "hexadecimal" characters. These characters include the alpha-numeric values of "A, B, C, D, E, F" and "0, 1, 2, 3, 4, 5, 6, 7, 8 and 9". Remember that any character viewed in a character format is only for the human eye. Computers actually use the "binary" equivalent any displayed character. Below are the listed hexadecimal characters associated with their binary equivalence:

Network Related Numbers Conversion		
Decimal	Hexadecimal	Binary
0	0	0000
1	1	0001
2	2	0010
3	3	0011
4	4	0100
5	5	0101
6	6	0110
7	7	0111
8	8	1000
9	9	1001
10	A	1010
11	B	1011
12	C	1100
13	D	1101
14	E	1110
15	F	1111

Let's look at the various formats and displays of the IPv6 format and characters. IPv6 addresses are written as a string of hexadecimal values. Take the following for example: 2001:1234:EF00:5678:9AAC:DDEE:FF11:ABCD

- Written in full form displays 32 hexadecimal characters.
    - o Every 4 bits = Single hexadecimal character.
- Total bits length is 128.
    - o Display is separated into eight sections separated by colons.
        - Example as in = $x^1{:}x^2{:}x^3{:}x^4{:}x^5{:}x^6{:}x^7{:}x^8$.
        - Each "x" = 16 bits in or four hexadecimal characters often called "Hextet" or "Hexword".

IPv6 Hexadecimal to Binary Conversions:

The following are some examples of how to read and convert the sections of a IPv6 IP address. We will keep it simple by using what is known as a "broadcast" IPv6 Address which reads as "FFFF:FFFF:FFFF:FFFF:FFFF:FFFF:FFFF:FFFF". You will notice that there are 8 sections which are separated by colons (:). Each sections is actually 16 binary "ones (1)". If the same address was displayed in binary, it would look like the following (For ease viewing, the 8 sections are separated into different colors.):

Counting all the bits from left to right, you notice that there are a total of 128-bits. When the bits are converted into hexadecimal, colons separate (:) every 16 bits creating 8 sections called "hextets" or "hexwords" as in "FFFF:FFFF:FFFF:FFFF:FFFF:FFFF:FFFF:FFFF". Each character (Not including the colons) represent the value of 4 binary characters. In the example we are using, each "F" is actually 4 binary "ones", as hexadecimal "F" = Binary "1111" and "Hexadecimal "FF" = binary "11111111". Let's take the explanation even further with the following examples:

- Hex FFFF = Binary of 1111111111111111
- Hex 0000 = Binary of 0000000000000000
- Hex D4DB = Binary of 1101010011011011

IPv6 Address Sections:

When using IPv6 it is required to understand the different sections included in the 128-bit identity. Similar to IPv4 sections which include a network section/ID, host section/ID and netmask indicator, IPv6 addresses have sections which provide similar functions but use different names. The following are the sections for IPv6:

- **Prefix** = Often times, internet service providers supply available IPv6 public addresses with the first 64 bits representing the entire network (Often indicated by "/64" appearing after the IP address). This requires every system on that network to have an identical collection of bits moving from the "Left-to-Right".
  - o Utilizes the bits moving from "Left-to-Right" (Often called the "Leftmost Bits").

- Devices on the same network will have a matching arrangement of "0's" and "1's" on the leftmost side.
- Expressed with a "/" similar to CIDR.
- Comparable to an IPv4 subnet mask.
- Examples of 4 systems in the same network would be as follows:
  - ➢ 2001:0db8:fd30:7654:1085:0099:fecc:5871 /64
  - ➢ 2001:0db8: fd30:7654:abcd:0052:e433:0001 /64
  - ➢ 2001:0db8: fd30:7654:dea0:8766:d222:98cc /64
  - ➢ 2001:0db8: fd30:7654:76ff:0433:5432:bb98 /64
    - ❖ The "/64" indicates that 1st 64 bits moving from "left-to-right" on all the nodes are identical.

- **Interface ID** = On a flat network, this will be the last 64bits of the IP address after the Prefix section. This section is used for the unique identifier of the specific node. Below, the section highlighted in "BOLD BLACK" would represent the interface ID. Examples of 4 systems in the same network would be as follows:
  - 2001:0db8:fd30:7654:1085:0099:fecc:5871 /64
  - 2001:0db8:fd30:7654:abcd:0052:e433:0001 /64
  - 2001:0db8:fd30:7654:dea0:8766:d222:98cc /64
  - 2001:0db8:fd30:7654:76ff:0433:5432:bb98 /64

IPv6 Written Format Methods:

Preferred Format = IPv6 addresses are very long in written format. This is what is called the "Preferred Format" which requires the display of all 32 hexadecimal characters. Below are examples of this format:
- 2001:0db8:0000:0000:0000:0578:abcd:00cb
- 2001:0000:abcd:0cbd:0000:321c:951d:fe35
- Fe80:1700:0000:00ce:0000:0000:0000:567d

Compressed Format = There are two options however which can be used to reduce the written/displayed characters of the IP address although all 128 bits are still being utilized. This method is referred to as "Compressed Format". The two methods are as follows:
- **Method #1** = Any leading hexadecimal 0's (zeros) in any 16-bit section (hextet) can be omitted:
- **Method #2** = Any string of one or more hexadecimal 0's (zeros) in a complete 16-bit segments (hextets) can be replaced with a zero (0) between colons or simply a double colon (::).

o The double colon (::) can only be used once within an address.
o This is commonly known as "Compressed Format".

Let's evaluate the method #1 which allows any leading hexadecimal zeros ("0's") in any 16-bit section (hextet) to be omitted. Using a single hextet example, notice how the method can be implemented:

- "01AB" can be written as "1AB"
- "09F0" can be written as "9F0"
- "0A00" can be written as "A00"
- "0000" can be written as ":0:"

Below are full text examples using the leading zero removal method:
- **Example 1:**
  o Preferred Format = 2001:0db8:0000:0000:0000:0578:abcd:00cb
  o Preceding Zero Removal Format = 2001:db8:0000:0000:0000:578:abcd:cb
- **Example 1:**
  o Preferred Format = 2001:0000:00cd:0cbd:0000:021c:951d:0035
  o Preceding Zero Removal Format = 2001:0000:cd:cbd:0000:21c:951d:35

Let's evaluate the method #2 which allows any string of one or more 16-bit segments (hextets) consisting of all 0's to be replaced with a zero between colons (:0:) or simply a double colon (::).
- Note: The double colon (::) can only be used once within an address.
- This is commonly known as "Compressed Format".
- Using a four hextet example, notice how the method can be implemented:
  o **"FE80:0000:0000:CD00"** can be written as **"FE80::CD00"**
  o **"FE80:1234:0000:0000"** can be written as **"FE80:1234:0:"**
  o **"FE80:0000:0000:0000"** can be written as **"FE80::"**

Below are additional examples using the Compression Method (Note, the syntax ": :" and can only be used once in a given IP address):

- **Preferred Format** = 2001:0db8:0000:0000:0000:0578:abcd:00cb
  o **Compressed Format** = 2001:0db8:0:0:0:0578:abcd:00cb
  o Or: 2001:0db8: :0578:abcd:00cb

- **Preferred Format** = 2001:0000:abcd:0cbd:0000:321c:951d:fe35
  - o **Compressed Format** = 2001: :abcd:0cbd:0:321c:951d:fe35

- **Preferred Format** = Fe80:1700:0000:00ce:0000:0000:0000:567d
  - o **Compressed Format** = Fe80:1700: :00ce:0:567d

Reserved IPv6 Addresses:

In IPv4, a number of IP addresses are classified as "Reserved" or "Special Use". A fast review of the following are examples:
- 169.254.x.y = Automatic Private IP Addressing.
- 127.0.0.1 = Local Host or Loopback Address
- 192.168.1.y = Internal private for testing and home networks.

IPv6 also has versions of IP addresses which provide similar functions although they have different names. Below are some of the special use IP addresses in IPv6. They are also matched with IPv4 types for easy comparison:

- **::/128 (Unspecified address)** = Indicates that the node does not have an IP address at present.
  - o Similar to "0.0.0.0" from IPv4.
- **::1/128 (Loopback)** = Used to test the configuration of TCP/IP on the local host.
  - o Similar to "127.0.0.1" from IPv4.

- **FC00::/ (Unique local)** = Local addressing within a site or between a limited number of sites.
  - o Similar to private IP addresses such as "172.16.x.y" and "192.168.x.y" from IPv4.

- **FE80:: (Link-local)** = Used to communicate with other devices on the same local network. Means that system has assigned itself an IP address
  - o Similar to "169.254.x.y" and APIPA from IPv4.

- **2001:: (Global unicast)** = Internet routable addresses accessible on the internet.
  - o This is the global unicast network prefix.
  - o Similar to a public IPv4 address.
  - o Static or dynamic.

- **FF00:(Multicast)** = Equivalent to the IPv4 224.x.x.x Class "D" addresses.

Displaying IPv6 Settings on Network Devices:

Depending on which type of device is on the network, there are various methods to view IP information. Windows-related systems have both a GUI method and command line method to review and make changes to IP information. Using Windows command line, some of the options is as follows:

- **Option #1 = ipconfig /all**

```
Administrator: C:\Windows\system32\cmd.exe

C:\>ipconfig /all

Windows IP Configuration

    Host Name . . . . . . . . . . . . : Unit04
    Primary Dns Suffix  . . . . . . . :
    Node Type . . . . . . . . . . . . : Hybrid
    IP Routing Enabled. . . . . . . . : No
    WINS Proxy Enabled. . . . . . . . : No

Wireless LAN adapter Wireless Network Connection 3:

    Media State . . . . . . . . . . . : Media disconnected
    Connection-specific DNS Suffix  . :
    Description . . . . . . . . . . . : Microsoft Virtual WiFi Miniport Adapter
    Physical Address. . . . . . . . . : 1C-3E-84-AF-4F-6F
    DHCP Enabled. . . . . . . . . . . : Yes
    Autoconfiguration Enabled . . . . : Yes

Wireless LAN adapter Wireless Network Connection 2:

    Connection-specific DNS Suffix  . :
    Description . . . . . . . . . . . : Dell Wireless 1504 802.11b/g/n (2.4GHz)
    Physical Address. . . . . . . . . : 1C-3E-84-AF-4F-6F
    DHCP Enabled. . . . . . . . . . . : Yes
    Autoconfiguration Enabled . . . . : Yes
    Link-local IPv6 Address . . . . . : fe80::b9d6:9590:92fb:3c8%15(Preferred)
    IPv4 Address. . . . . . . . . . . : 192.168.1.128(Preferred)
    Subnet Mask . . . . . . . . . . . : 255.255.255.0
    Lease Obtained. . . . . . . . . . : Thursday, March 09, 2017 8:05:59 AM
    Lease Expires . . . . . . . . . . : Thursday, March 09, 2017 10:20:59 AM
    Default Gateway . . . . . . . . . : 192.168.1.10
    DHCP Server . . . . . . . . . . . : 192.168.1.24
```

- **Option #2 = netstat –r**

```
C:\Windows\system32\cmd.exe

      10.10.40.0      255.255.248.0         On-link        10.10.41.8    276
      10.10.41.8    255.255.255.255         On-link        10.10.41.8    276
    10.10.47.255    255.255.255.255         On-link        10.10.41.8    276
       127.0.0.0          255.0.0.0         On-link         127.0.0.1    306
       127.0.0.1    255.255.255.255         On-link         127.0.0.1    306
 127.255.255.255    255.255.255.255         On-link         127.0.0.1    306
       224.0.0.0          240.0.0.0         On-link         127.0.0.1    306
       224.0.0.0          240.0.0.0         On-link        10.10.41.8    276
 255.255.255.255    255.255.255.255         On-link         127.0.0.1    306
 255.255.255.255    255.255.255.255         On-link        10.10.41.8    276
===========================================================================
Persistent Routes:
  None

IPv6 Route Table
===========================================================================
Active Routes:
 If Metric Network Destination      Gateway
  1    306 ::1/128                  On-link
  1    306 ff00::/8                 On-link
===========================================================================
Persistent Routes:
  None

C:\Users\rspencer>
```

When accessing corporate routers or switches. There is only a GUI option if the device is fully configured. If not, a terminal emulator such as Teraterm, Putty or HyperTerminal must be used. The following command would be used:
- **show ipv6 interface brief (Example is displayed below):**

```
Router#show ipv6 interface brief
FastEthernet0/0                [administratively down/down]
    FE80::2E0:A3FF:FEAE:5301
    2001:44:7455:ABCD:9855::1
```

Configuring IPv6 addresses on Routers:

IPv6 routing is not enabled by default. To enable a router to utilize IPv6 on its interfaces, you have to activate the service on the router. In order to do this, you must perform the following as an IPv6 router:
- "Router (config)# ipv6 unicast-routing"

After configuring the router for IPv6, it is now possible to add IP settings to individual interfaces. The process and commands to complete this task appear below (Note: Compressed format is used in this example):
- **Router(config)#interface fa0/0**
- **Router(config-if)# ipv6 add 2001:0044:7455:abcd:9855::1/32**
- **Router(config-if)#no shutdown**

Subnetting IPv6 Methods and Exercises:

The process of subnetting for IPv4 is done to more efficiently utilize IP address. Due the design of IPv6, there is really no need to subdivide networks. It is sometimes desirable, however to separate sections of networks for security reasons. Under this type of situation, subnetting can also be done on IPv6 networks. In order to utilize subnetting on IPv6 networks it is necessary to modify the identity sections of the address using the following terms:

IPv6 Sections (Total 128 Bits)		
Global Routing Prefix (48bits)	Subnet ID (16Bits)	Interface Identifier (64Bits)

- **Global Routing Prefix**= Traditionally the first 4 hextets (Total of 64 Bits) on IPv6 networks which are not subnetted. The display below in binary and highlighted in BLACK BOLD displays a site Prefix:

  11111111.11111111.11111111.11111111 11111111.0000000000000000.0000000000000000.0000000000000000. 0000000000000000

When subnetting IPv6 networks, traditionally the third hextet is utilized which reduces the size of the site prefix to the 1st 48 bits of the IP address as follows:

- **Site Prefix** = Section of the Global Routing prefix reduced to the 1st 48 bits or 1st three hextets in order to perform subnetting:

  1111111111111111.1111111111111111.1111111111111111.00000000 00000000.0000000000000000.0000000000000000.0000000000000000 .0000000000000000

- **Subnet ID** = The 4th hextet (Total of 16 bits from 49th to the 64th bit):

  0000000000000000.0000000000000000.0000000000000000.**11111111 11111111**.0000000000000000.0000000000000000.0000000000000000 .0000000000000000

The remainder of the IPv6 IP address is still classified as the "Host" or "Interface ID" (64th to 128th bit or simply the last four hextets).

  0000000000000000.0000000000000000.0000000000000000. 0000000000000000.**1111111111111111. 1111111111111111. 1111111111111111. 1111111111111111**

There are a number of ways to perform the subnetting process. In this text, we will evaluate three as in the following:
- IPv6 Subnet Table.
- Subnet ID.
- Subnetting on a "Nibble".

IPv6 Subnet Table = Using the "IP6 Subnet Section Table" from the Spencer Method we can utilize the same method which was used for subnetting IPv4 networks. The same scale of numbers is used except that the scale has the potential to increase to a total of 16 value areas.

IPv6 Subnet Section Table														
(H-2)	4	8	16	32	64	128	256	512	1024	2048	4096	8192	16384	32768	65536

Each area represents one of the bits in the Subnet ID. Let's look at the following examples:

- A computer has the IP address "2001:3d6c:abcd:0cbd:0:321c:951d:fe35".
- What is required to make sure that subnet can support 1000 networks with 60 hosts on each?
  o Answer = 2001:3d6c:abcd:FE00:0cbd:321c:951d:fe35

The question above requires us to use a process similar to IPv4 subnetting, it is recommended that you break the questions into the following sequence of operations (H,N,H = Find Hosts then Networks, then answer in hexadecimal). Let's work the problem:
- Identify the 4th section of the original IP address (Subnet ID – Listed in BOLD BLACK:
  o 2001:3d6c:abcd:0cbd:0000:321c:951d:fe35

To get 60 hosts:
- Use "IPv6 Subnet Table" chart to move up to "64" which results in a usable total of "62".

IPv6 Subnet Section Table														
(H-2)	4	8	16	32	64	128	256	512	1024	2048	4096	8192	16384	32768	65536
X	X	X	X	X	X										

- Count the spaces up to and including "64" which equals "6" spaces".
- Write out six zeros from right-to left resulting in "000000".
  o The binary "0's" will allow you to have the required amount of hosts.
- Add enough binary "1's" to the left of the last zero on the left to render a total of sixteen binary characters as in "1111111111000000".
  o The binary "1's" will allow you to have the required amount of subnets.
- Moving from left to right, temporarily insert a "dash (-)" between every "four" bits as in the following "1111-1111-1100-0000".

- Convert each section separated by the dashes into the hexadecimal value:
  - 1111 = F
  - 1110 = E
  - 1100 = B
  - 0000 = 0
- Replace the subnet IP with the above which provides the answer:
  - 2001:3d6c:abcd:fec0:0000:321c:951d:fe35

Let's try another:
- A computer has the IP address "2001:cefd:876c:0cbd:ad7f:321c:951d:fe35". What is required to make sure that subnet can support 45 networks with 900 hosts on each?
  - Answer = 2001:3d6c:abcd:fc00:0000:321c:951d:fe35

Remember the sequence of operations (H,N,H = Find Hosts then Networks, then answer in hexadecimal). Let's work the problem:
- Identify the 4th section to use for subnetting (Subnet ID – Listed in **BOLD BLACK**):
  - 2001:cefd:876c:**0cbd**:ad7f:321c:951d:fe35"

To get 900 hosts:
- Use "IPv6 Subnet Table" chart to move up to "1024" which results in a usable total of "1022".

IPv6 Subnet Section Table															
(H-2)	4	8	16	32	64	128	256	512	1024	2048	4096	8192	16384	32768	65536
X	X	X	X	X	X	X	X	X	X						

- Count the spaces up to and including "1024" which equals "10" spaces".
- Write out ten zeros from right-to left resulting in "0000000000".
  - The binary "0's" will allow you to have the required amount of hosts.
- Add enough binary "1's" to the left of the last zero on the left to render a total of sixteen binary characters as in "1111110000000000".
  - The binary "1's" will allow you to have the required amount of subnets.
- Moving from left to right, temporarily insert a "dash (-)" between every "four" bits as in the following "1111-1100-0000-0000".

- Convert each section separated by the dashes into the hexadecimal value:
  - 1111 = F
  - 1100 = C
  - 0000 = 0
  - 0000 = 0
- Replace the subnet IP with the above which provides the answer:
  - 2001:3d6c:abcd:fc00:0000:321c:951d:fe35

Subnet Block ID Method = This method is less detailed than the Spencer method. Instead of developing subnets based on specific numbers of nodes and networks, utilizing the values of the hexadecimal characters, it is possible to simply create differentiated subnets and then place a router between them if inter-network communication is needed. This is done simply by creating an arbitrary Subnet ID and incrementing the hextet by the next higher last character. The following would be an example:

- Assigned network Global Prefix (Compressed Format) = 2001:cefd:876c:0cbd::/32
  - Subnet ID section highlighted in BOLD BLACK = 2001:cefd:876c:0cbd::/48

- Subnet ID section modified for networks = 2001:cefd:876c:0000::/48
- Creating subnets by increasing the hextet:
  - 1st network = 2001:cefd:876c:0001::/48
  - 2nd network = 2001:cefd:876c:0002::/48
  - 3rd network = 2001:cefd:876c:0003::/48
  - Continue until you hit the last value for the 4th hextet "FFFF"
    - 2001:cefd:876c:FFFF::/48

Subnetting on a "Nibble" Method = Although traditionally, when subnetting IPv6 the 4th octet is used (Subnet ID), it is actually possible to use any leading section of the last 64 bits as long as enough bits remain at the tail end of the interface ID section to create distinct node identifiers. This method is called "Subnetting on a Nibble". The process allows the creation of subnets by modifying the 5th octet in 4-bit increases. This in turn, changes the netmask indicator (The "/" number at the end of the IPv6 address). Take the following examples:

- **Assigned network Global Prefix** = 2001:cefd:876c:0cbd:0:0:0:0:/64
  - Interface ID section highlighted in GREY =
    2001:cefd:876c:0cbd:0:0:0:0/64
  - Hex character used for subnetting in BLACK BOLD=
    2001:cefd:876c:0cbd:0000:0:0:0/64

- Creating subnets by increasing the 5th hex character (BOLD BLACK)
  moving from right-to-left:
  - 1st network = 2001:cefd:876c:0cbd:1000:0:0:0/68
  - 2nd network = 2001:cefd:876c:0cbd:2000:0:0:0/68
  - 3rd network = 2001:cefd:876c:0cbd:3000:0:0:0/68

As you can see, "Subnetting-on-a-Nibble" is not a method to create a specific number of hosts or subnets, but it does guarantee divisions between sections of a network. As a Cisco technology professional, it is up to you to select the best option to address the needs of the organization for which you are employed.

Conclusion of the book:

You have reached the end of this text and I hope it has benefited you greatly. In the writing of this book, it was my desire to impart knowledge and methods which readers could use to increase their understanding of network technology. In addition, many sections are directly dedicated to both building network infrastructures as well as gaining network technology-related certifications. I hope you have benefited from my work and I wish you great success in all your adventures in network technology. Remember,…"Knowledge First in All Matters!!!!"

CPSIA information can be obtained
at www.ICGtesting.com
Printed in the USA
LVHW021508201220
674691LV00009B/508

9 781798 861073